SHINTOISM

THE INDIGENOUS RELIGION OF JAPAN

BY

A. C. UNDERWOOD, M.A., D.D.

Principal of Rawdon College, Leeds

T0283065

CONTENTS

5

LIST OF ABBREVIATIONS USED

Anesaki . . . *History of Japanese Religion* (London, 1930).

Aston,S.A.R.J. . *Shinto, the Ancient Religion of Japan* (London, 1921).

Aston, S.W.G. . *Shinto, the Way of the Gods* (London, 1905).

E.R.E. . . . *Encyclopædia of Religion and Ethics.*

Griffis . . . . *The Religions of Japan* (London, 1895).

Kato . . . . *A Study of Shinto* (Tokyo, 1926).

Knox . . . . *The Development of Religion in Japan* (London, 1907).

EDITOR'S FOREWORD

THE quest for God is one in which all nations have shared. Call Him what they may, all peoples seek God, though they seek not as do we. Yet to understand both their unity with and differences from us must help to closer sympathy and respect. The purpose of this series is not critical nor apologetic, but rather is it descriptive. It is that of giving some account, by reference to the scriptures and great teachers of other religions, of the way in which the faiths of the world have faced the same spiritual issues that are ours. In this respect they are intended as a simply written contribution to the work of the Comparative Study of Religions.

E.S.W.

PREFACE

Books on Shinto are not numerous. The best of them are out of print and are, therefore, difficult to secure. This volume has been written in the hope that it will make a clear account of Shinto readily accessible to the student who may easily be daunted by the inherent difficulties of the subject. It makes no claim to originality. Any one who writes on Shinto must avail himself freely of the labours of Aston and Revon. This I have done. The student will find a short annotated Bibliography at the end of this work.

I am indebted to my colleague, Dr. George Howells, for reading my manuscript and making valuable suggestions; and to Miss Hargreaves for preparing a clean type-script.

A. C. UNDERWOOD.

SHINTOISM

CHAPTER I

INTRODUCTORY

To provide the student with a background against which to set his study of Shintoism, a summary account is given in this chapter of Japan, its people and its history.

Japan, called by its own people Nippon, comprises a group of more than forty islands and a great number of islets, which lie off the eastern coast of Asia. About five hundred islands, large and small, are inhabited. Japan is a country of high mountain ranges, many volcanoes, deep valleys, few plains, no great rivers and frequent earthquakes. The deeply indented coastline makes the ratio of coastline to land-area higher than that of Greece or Norway.

Though the climate ranges from sub-tropical to sub-arctic, it is, on the whole, kind and the people are able to live much in the open-air amid fields which are bright with grasses and flowers almost throughout the year. ' The blue waters of the many bays and inlets, the gentle slopes of the mountains, the graceful curves of the volcanoes, and the abrupt promontories overgrown with fantastic trees, these picturesque scenes cannot fail to awaken in a responsive heart a tender love for nature. These natural blessings remain ever a benignant influence upon the sentimental life of the nation.'[1] Indeed the Japanese appreciated the æsthetic appeal of snow-capped mountains much earlier than did the nations of Europe. ' Why for thousands of years did no one in Europe see the beauty of a wild mountain landscape, until a century and a half ago ? . . . Twice Luther walked through Switzerland without seeing the glory of the Alps. Elsewhere he always had eyes to see with. It was not until Rousseau and Romanticism that the West was taught the splendours of the Alpine world.'[2]

The Japanese people are of a mixed stock. The ethnological problems of their origin are not yet settled, but it is clear that they are the result of a fusion of various immigrant peoples with the original inhabitants, represented to-day by the Ainus, who are now found only in the northern parts of Japan. The chief immigrants were Manchu-Koreans and Mongolians from the mainland and Malayans from the south. All these strains are found among the Japanese of to-day. Within the last sixty years the population has doubled ; it is now roughly sixty-six millions and is still rapidly increasing.

The peculiar geographical position and the historical development of the Japanese Empire have made its people patriotic to the verge of chauvinism. Everything they adopt they adjust to their own needs. Their genius shows itself in adaptation rather than in original creation ; but, as Mr. Basil Mathews points out, their power of selective imitation and syncretistic adaptation is such that, in the long run, they make a new creation out of borrowed ideas. The history of Buddhism in Japan is an excellent illustration of this point.

[1] Anesaki, p. 5.   [2] Soderblom, *The Living God*, p. 358.

Of the ancient history of Japan little can be said definitely and in detail, because the native annals are so thickly encrusted with legend. It is, however, clear that in the earliest times the land was peopled with numerous tribes, in which the trades and professions were all hereditary. Conditions were primitive ; the land and the people belonged to the tribal chief. Gradually the tribes coalesced into a united people under an emperor. It is impossible to determine precisely the date at which this political unification took place. According to the native records the first Emperor (Mikado) was Jimmu, who is said to have succeeded to the throne in 660 B.C. ; but there are difficulties in the way of accepting this tradition as authentic. From Jimmu the present Emperor traces his descent in an unbroken line. During this period Shinto, as it came to be called, took shape and remained the only religion of Japan prior to the introduction of Buddhism.

Culture and the arts of civilization first came to Japan in the middle of the sixth century A.D. from the Chinese mainland. They came in with Buddhism and great advances in civilization followed. The new religion brought with it the arts, literature, civic morality, legal institutions and educational methods. The acceptance of these helped to consolidate that national unity which had been achieved at an earlier date. The supremacy of Shinto was challenged ; for Buddhism was adopted and fostered by successive emperors.

From A.D. 800 to A.D. 1200 we have an age of peace and ease, known as the Period of Heian, remarkable for the development of the sects of Japanese Buddhism.

This was followed by the Period of Feudal Strife,

which lasted from 1200 to 1600. During this period
the Emperor was unable to control the military classes,
who by 1200 had risen to power. It was a period of
confusion during which civil war ravaged the land with
fire and sword. The confusion was aggravated by the
introduction of Christianity by Jesuit missionaries in
the middle of the sixteenth century. A little later,
in 1549, Francis Xavier arrived and spent twenty-seven
months in Japan. Many converts to Christianity were
made and it is said that by the year 1596 they numbered
as many as 300,000. From 800 to 1700 Buddhism was
the established religion and enjoyed the powerful
support of the court. To all intents and purposes
Shinto was amalgamated with its rival, thus producing
Ryobu or Mixed Shinto.

Next followed the Tokugawa Régime of peace and
order (1600 to 1868). It is so called after the Tokugawa
family in whose hands the power remained throughout
the whole period. They provided the Shoguns.
Shogun means generalissimo or Commander-in-Chief.
Each Shogun was ceremonially invested with authority
by the Emperor ; but in point of fact the Emperor was
a mere puppet, the Shogun being the *de facto* ruler of
the country and exercising dictatorial power over the
feudal states. The Shoguns ' adopted a definitely
centralizing policy, designed to prevent the rise of any
political or social factor to unmanageable magnitude.'
Early in this period a bitter persecution of the
Christians broke out. The Japanese were suspicious
that the real object of the missionaries was to gain
possession of Japan for the European nations. The
missionaries were, therefore, expelled and Christianity
suppressed. Fiendish tortures were applied to secure
recantations and many native Christians apostatized.

For more than two centuries Japan was closed to all foreigners. In 1854, however, Commodore Perry succeeded in negotiating a treaty between the United States of America and Japan, which led to subsequent treaties, one of which allowed foreigners to live in certain ports. Both Roman and Protestant missionaries took advantage of the opening thus offered and soon descendants of the ancient Christians were found. It was not until 1889 that liberty of conscience was granted by the government. During the Tokugawa Period falls the indigenous revival of Shinto which is treated below in a separate chapter.

In 1868 the Shogunate was overthrown and the Mikado was restored to his ancient place and power. In that year began the present Meiji Era—the Era of Enlightenment. Soon after the Restoration of 1868 the leading Samurai, who had strongly opposed the opening of the ports by the Shogunate, adopted a progressive and Europeanizing policy. The Japanese again deliberately absorbed an alien culture and by adopting the scientific, industrial, military and naval techniques of the West became ' the Asiatic spearhead of mechanistic civilization.' The Restoration naturally brought Shinto again to the front but it soon subsided into inertia, though in its sectarian forms it has manifested a new religious vitality of great interest.

CHAPTER II

SOURCES AND
GENERAL CHARACTERISTICS

SHINTO is the indigenous religion of Japan. Its beginnings are lost in the mists of antiquity but it is clear that it began as a form of nature-worship. At a later date were added the cult of the Emperor and the worship of ancestors. The history of Shinto is bound up, as we shall see, with the fluctuating history of religion in Japan.

Shinto means 'The Way of the Gods'—the last syllable being the Chinese ' Tao.' Shinto is the Chinese equivalent of the Japanese *Kami no michi*, which means ' The Way of the Superior Beings '—the ' no ' being the possessive. The indigenous religion of Japan did not receive the name Shinto until it became necessary to distinguish it from Buddhism (Butsudo), which had been imported into Japan with Chinese civilization.

For our knowledge of the earliest forms of Shinto we are dependent upon the following written sources : (1) The *Kojiki* ('Records of Ancient Matters') is written in mingled archaic Japanese and Chinese. It was compiled in A.D. 712 at the command of an Emperor who was afraid that the many variants then in existence might destroy ' ere many years shall elapse the great basis of the country and the grand foundation of the monarchy.' The *Kojiki* has some-times been called ' The Bible of the Japanese,' but it is difficult to find a religious motive behind its compilation, save in so far as it sets forth the old stories of the ' origin of deities and the establishment of men.' The predominant aim of the compilation was to demonstrate the divine origin of the ruling family and the remote antiquity of the foundation of the State. Japan is to be like China ; she, too, is to have a cosmogony, a national history and an account of how the Ruling House obtained its power.[1]   The suggestion that the *Kojiki* is the Japanese Bible overlooks the fact that there is in Shinto no collection of sacred writings regarded as canonical or as authoritative for doctrine and ethics.   The *Kojiki* is not regarded as inspired nor can it be said to possess any devotional interest.   In 1882 B. H. Chamberlain published in Tokyo a translation of the *Kojiki* in *Transactions of the Asiatic Society of Japan*, which was reprinted in 1906 and 1920.

(2).   The *Nihongi* (' Chronicles of Japan ') was compiled in A.D. 720.   Written wholly in Chinese, it covers in part the same ground as the *Kojiki* and contains alternative versions of the same myth or event.   A Translation of the *Nihongi* by W. G. Aston appeared in 1896 (London) in *Transactions and Proceedings of the Japan Society* and was reprinted in 1924.

(3).   The *Yengi-shiki* (' Institutes of the Yengi Period ') describes the ritual as practised in the Yengi Era (901–923) and includes some prayers (*norito*) which have come down from very ancient times.   It is, therefore, a valuable source of information for the ceremonies of Shinto.   Translations of some of the *norito* are given by Aston in his *Shinto, the Way of the Gods*.

[1] cf. Anesaki, p. 87, and Knox, p. 57.

(4). The *Manyo-shiu* ('Collection of Myriad Leaves')
is a collection of four hundred poems compiled towards
the end of the eighth century or at the beginning of
the ninth. 'The collection represents the poetic
genius of a people just emerging from a primitive
outlook and aspiring towards deeper sentiments and
higher ideals.'[1] A translation of 264 of the poems
may be found in Dickins' *Primitive and Mediæval
Japanese Texts* (Oxford, 1906). In view of the fact
that Shinto is fundamentally a form of nature-worship,
it is worth pointing out that the *Manyo-shiu* contains
a number of lyrical poems which celebrate all the
splendours of the Japanese landscape from the smallest
herb of the plain up to the lofty summit of Mount
Fujiyama.

The religion reflected in the earliest strata of the
above sources belongs to the childhood of the race,
when 'the trees and herbs had speech' as the *Nihongi*
says. All is rudimentary and unorganized. We find
an amazing number of deities but look in vain for a
system of doctrine or of morals. Of metaphysical
background there is not a vestige. Nor is there any
discussion of those great themes of which all great
religious literature treats, such as the problem of evil,
man's consciousness of sin and his need of redemption.
'It was a fairy world taken as matter of fact, with all
distinctions between the possible and the impossible
wanting.'[2] Crocodiles became women; men became
birds; fishes, beasts, birds and serpents acted and
spoke like men. Heaven was so near to earth that
an arrow shot from the earth made a hole in the
bottom of it through which objects fell which are still
found upon the earth. Spirits, both good and evil,

[1] Anesaki, p. 101, who gives a few examples. [2] Knox, p. 19.

were supposed to exist everywhere and Shinto was an unorganized worship of these deities and spirits.

The name which is given in Shinto to all deities and spirits is *Kami*—an important term, the significance of which needs to be defined for a proper understanding of Shinto. *Kami*[1] is used of anything possessing supernatural power or force. It is, therefore, applied to all supernatural beings (whether good or evil), to the spirits of the departed and to natural objects which possess extraordinary features. It is usual to cite the following passage from the writings of Motoöri, a distinguished Shintoist theologian of the eighteenth century, as the best available definition of *Kami*.

' The term *Kami* is applied in the first place to the various deities of Heaven and Earth, who are mentioned in the ancient records as well as to their spirits (*mitama*) which reside in the shrines where they are worshipped. Moreover, not only human beings, but birds, beasts, plants and trees, seas and mountains, and all other things whatsoever which deserve to be dreaded and revered for the extraordinary and pre-eminent powers which they possess, are called *Kami*. They need not be eminent for surpassing nobleness, goodness, or serviceableness alone. Malignant and uncanny beings are also called *Kami* if only they are the objects of general dread. Among *Kami* who are human beings I need hardly mention first of all the successive Mikados—with reverence be it spoken. . . . Then there have been numerous examples of divine beings, both in ancient and modern times, who, although not accepted by the nation generally, are treated as gods, each of his several dignity, in a single province, village or family . . . Among *Kami* who are not human beings, I need hardly mention Thunder. There are also the Dragon, the Echo, and the Fox, who are *Kami* by reason of their uncanny and fearful natures. The term *Kami* is applied in the *Nihongi* and *Manyo-shiu* to the tiger and wolf . . . There are many cases of seas and mountains being called

1 For the derivation of the word *Kami* and the various definitions of it given in modern Japanese dictionaries see E.R.E. VI, pp. 294f.

2

Kami. It is not their spirits which are meant. The word was applied directly to the seas or mountains themselves as being very awful beings.' [1]

As a convenient summary definition of *Kami* we may accept that offered by Knox. 'All that is wonderful is God, and the divine embraces in its category all that impresses the untrained imagination and excites it to reverence or fear.' [2]

From the above quotation it will be seen that Shinto is incurably polytheistic and is able to create new *Kami* from time to time. Dr. Nitobe does not hesitate to say that 'Shinto is the most polytheistic of polytheisms.' [3] Its deities range, he says, from the most insignificant gods 'whom pious spinsters respect as the spirits of sewing-needles or those to whom kitchen-maids do homage as residing in the furnace, up to those who roar in thunder, or shine in lightning, or ride upon the whirlwind.'

Especially were the awe-inspiring phenomena of nature and her mysterious processes selected by Shinto as objects of worship. The sky, the heavenly bodies, the mountains, the rivers and the seas are all venerated as divine ; so, too, are trees, beasts, birds, great fishes and reptiles as well as the process of reproduction in nature and in man. There was a somewhat similar nature-worship in the earliest days in China but Krause points out [4] the rise and development of the cult was entirely different in the two countries. In China nature-worship arose as the result of the observation of nature and from the desire to include human life in the great harmony manifested in the universe. In Japan it was ' the child of the youthful imagination

---

[1] Quoted by Aston. S.W.G., pp. 8f.   [2] Knox, p. 31.
[3] *The Japanese Nation*, p. 131.
[4] In Clemen's *Religions of the World*, p. 254.

that knows nothing of logic. The first expression of Japanese thought is the fairy-tale.' This point will be clearer after we have considered the Mythology of Shinto, and if we remember that Japan owed her civilization to China, and that in the days with which we are now dealing Chinese cultural and religious influences had not yet made themselves felt upon the life of Japan. Shinto is not, therefore, an exalted form of nature-worship but rather a parcelling out of nature among many deities, who are conceived in a thorough-going anthropomorphic fashion. They are thought of as living and acting exactly like Japanese. All is popular and unsophisticated and entirely without system.

In the seventh century, however, this amorphous system gained something like shape and coherence by being related to the Emperor, who was set forth in the *Kojiki* as a direct descendant of the Sun-goddess. By that time the dynasty, which still reigns over Japan, had obtained power over the greater part of the previously disorganized country. In order to bind the people to the reigning house the old myths were retold and elaborated and the Emperor himself was declared to be divine. In the *Kojiki* it is shown how the Emperor can trace his descent from the Sun-goddess (Amaterasu) and through her from Izanagi and Izanami, the two primal deities who gave birth to all the other gods and to the islands of Japan. This elaboration and organization of the nature-worship of Shinto in the interests of the reigning house is the really characteristic feature of Shinto in historic times and has given to Shinto its typically national form. It also explains why the worship of the Sun-goddess has become prominent throughout the country.

' In the homage paid to the divine emperor the religion of the Japanese nation thus found a centre of gravity that gradually attracted all the centrifugal elements of its varied pantheon and its world of spirits.'[1]

The question whether ancestor-worship has formed part of Shinto from the earliest days is one upon which opinion is divided. When the study of Shinto was first undertaken by European scholars they usually declared that the twin bases of Shinto from the earliest times were nature-worship and ancestor-worship.[2] This opinion was firmly maintained by the native Shintoist scholars who led the revival of Shinto in the eighteenth century. It is also defended by a modern Shintoist scholar, Dr. Genchi Kato, who says that ' the origin of Japanese religion partakes of both nature-worship and ancestor-worship.'[3] But recent Western scholarship definitely inclines to the view that ancestor-worship was not indigenous to Japan but came in with Chinese influences.[4] These scholars draw a distinction, which was not so clear fifty years ago, between the cult of the dead and the cult of ancestors. They do not deny that in early Shinto there was a cult of the dead, based on the fear that the dead would do mischief to the living if they were neglected by them. They point out, however, that true ancestor-worship involves a conception of a spiritual fraternity and that in it offerings are made to departed ancestors not merely through fear but in order to promote the prosperity of, as well as to secure protection for, the family or clan. In the early religion of China there

---

[1] Krause in Clemen's *Religions of the World*, p. 258.
[2] *e.g.* Griffis, p. 88.   [3] Kato, p. 53.
[4] See Aston, S.W.G., pp. 44ff ; Knox, pp. 27, 66f ; Moore, *History of Religions*, Vol. I, pp. 110ff ; and Revon in E.R.E. I, p. 455ff.

is found a true form of ancestor-worship based upon the conception of an enlarged family which includes both the living and the dead and upon the desire to find a place for departed souls in a unified nature charged with all manner of potencies. In the earliest days in Japan, however, this conception of an enlarged family is wanting and the cult of the dead is based upon fear of the dead and the desire to be separated from them. Western scholars further point out that prior to the sixth century A.D. there is no evidence of the worship even of the Emperor's ancestors. References to such worship are rare in the *Kojiki* and the *Nihongi*, though it is prescribed by the *Yengi-shiki*, which belongs to the tenth century.

We conclude, then, that early Shinto was an unorganized worship of nature and spirits which included a vague cult of the dead such as is common among all animistic peoples. At a later date and under Chinese influences a genuine ancestor-worship arose and the spirits of departed ancestors took their place beside the *Kami* and with them received a veneration which was based on something more than fear. In this and in other connexions it is important to bear in mind that our knowledge of Japan before it came under Chinese influences is very meagre and that every description of the earliest forms of Shinto must, in the nature of things, be largely a reconstruction based on fragmentary evidence, all of which has been affected by Chinese influences. ' We must also keep in mind that within historical times there has never really been a pure Shinto or a pure Buddhism (in Japan) and that at all periods we find mixed forms and variations on the same theme.'[1] There is, therefore, some point in

[1] Krause in Clemen, *op. cit.*, p. 259.

Dr. Kato's question, ' Who can prove with historical certainty that ancestor-worship is utterly absent in ancient Japan ? ' [1] In this matter there is no such thing as historical certainty. When, however, scholarship has divested Shinto of the foreign elements in which it became entangled, all the probabilities point to the conclusion that Primitive Shinto had no true ancestor-worship but a vague cult of the dead, which was afterwards elaborated and systematized under Chinese influences into a genuine cult of ancestors.

[1] Kato, p. 53.

CHAPTER III

MYTHOLOGY AND COSMOGONY

THE *Kojiki* is our chief authority for the mythology and cosmogony of Shinto. It takes us back to prehistoric times when men had no conception of cosmic order and natural law and, being unable to distinguish between history and fable, they were impressed by and contented with the grotesque and fanciful. Many of the myths of the *Kojiki* are repeated with variations in the *Nihongi* and most of them were amplified to such an extent that it is now not always easy to discover the purpose they were designed to serve and the questions they were intended to answer.

There is a cycle of myths familiar to students of the primitive forms of religion and dealing with primeval chaos and the beginnings of life. Three deities are said to have sprung out of primeval chaos which is likened to an ocean of mud veiled in darkness. This first triad vanishes without leaving any posterity. Then while the earth was young and was drifting about like oil floating on water, two more heavenly deities were born. These also vanish leaving no descendants behind. Two more heavenly deities then appear and disappear and finally five couples emerge, with the last of whom, Izanagi and Izanami, the myth begins. The gods prior to Izanagi and Izanami are usually called the celestial deities to distinguish them from the earthly deities, who are said to have walked on the earth. Some scholars think these heavenly deities

23

may have been deities no longer worshipped in Japan. It is more likely that they were mere inventions to eke out a genealogical tree for the greater divinities who come afterwards.[1] The real cosmogonic deities are Izanagi and Izanami. The gods who are mentioned as existing prior to them merely serve to give the Divine Pair a pedigree of respectable length.[2]

Izanagi (the Male-who-Invites) and Izanami (the Female-who-Invites) were ordered by the celestial deities to descend to earth in order to produce the terrestrial world. ' These two at the command of the heavenly deities stood on the Floating Bridge of Heaven, pushed down the jewelled spear, which had been given them, stirred up the brine beneath till it went curdle-curdle, and drew the spear up, the brine which dripped from it piling up and forming the island called " Self-Curdling." Descending they erect a pillar and a hall, and then begins their courtship. Circling the island, when they meet she exclaims, " O beautiful and amiable youth ! " and he responds, " O beautiful and amiable maiden ! " This institutes their courtship, and after marriage which is without ceremony, or negotiations or capture, are born the islands, the plains, the elements and the forces of nature. Their first child was a failure, and the second, the island of Awa (Foam), also, because Izanami spoke first on their meeting . . . and therefore the courtship is repeated and Izanagi first makes the exclamation, " Ah ! What a fair and lovely maiden ! " and then after her response the work of creation prospers. The geography known by the middle of the seventh century is given in detail, the various islands of the archipelago,

[1] See Aston. S.A.R.J., p. 20 and Anesaki, p. 24.
[2] cf. Moore, *History of Religions*, Vol. I, p. 98.

the great central country of Yamato. After the geography is complete come deities which are objects and forces of nature, Deity Rock Earth Prince, Heavenly Blowing Male, Youth of the Wind Breath the Great Male, the Spring, the Summer, the Autumn, Foam Calm, Foam Waves, Bubble Calm, Bubble Waves, Wind and Trees, and Mountains and Moors and Passes, and Food and Fire. The total number of islands begotten was fourteen, and of other deities thirty-five . . . So far then the nature of the story is clear, a myth to explain the beginnings of marriage, and the birth, in human fashion, of islands, and mountains and rocks, and trees, and elements—all ætiological, with perhaps only the Bridge of Heaven, the courtship, and stories of the marriage of the nature of true legend.'[1] We may, perhaps, also see in the myth evidence that the matriarchal state of society was just passing away. Disaster followed when Izanami spoke first on meeting her spouse. All went well when the courtship was renewed and Izanagi spoke the first word. The myth appears to show why the man should have the precedence.[2]

These fanciful stories of the creation of Japan and of the mountains, fields, mist, fire and so on, are told with complete naïveté. All are begotten precisely as men and animals beget their offspring. All the things produced were called *Kami*.

In giving birth to Fire, Izanami died and went to the nether world. Whereupon Izanagi kills the Fire Prince with his sword and from the blood which drips from the blade eight more deities are born. Izanagi then follows his wife to Hades where he finds her decaying body swarming with maggots and eight

[1] Knox, pp. 59-61.   [2] cf. Knox, p. 14.

thunder gods born in her body and dwelling there. Though Izanami is a mass of corruption she is still conscious and capable of anger and vengeance. ' For she orders the ugly female of Hades to pursue him ; but fleeing, he casts down his head-dress, which turns to grapes, which tempt her and she stops to eat. As she again pursues, he throws down his comb, which turns into bamboo shoots, and she stops again to pull and eat them. Then the wife sends forth thunder gods, which she had begotten in her filth ; but he threatens them with his sword and defeats them by pelting them with peaches. Finally Izanami arouses herself and comes after him, catching him just as he passes the Even Pass of Hades, which he blocks with a great rock. When over it, safe from further pursuit, he divorces her, and after mutual challenges they separate, he to purify himself and she to become the great deity of Hades.'[1]

The story is evidently designed to show that death is the necessary counterpart of life. The divine couple were the originators of life but the myth shows how the Female-who-Invites became the genius of evil and death and how she tried to confine the Male in the realm of darkness and death.

The cosmogony is completed with stories of the birth of the Sun, the Moon and the Rain-Storm god. According to one version of the myth all three were begotten in the usual manner by the Divine Pair, Izanagi and Izanami. According to another tradition, these three deities were born when Izanagi was washing away in the sea the stains he had incurred during his visit to Hades. The Sun-goddess (Amaterasu) was washed from the filth which filled Izanagi's right eye.

[1] Knox, p. 19f.

The Sun-goddess is the mightiest of the hosts of heaven and is now the most important object of worship among the nature-deities of Shinto. The Moon-god (Tsuki-yomi) was washed from the filth that filled Izanagi's left eye and the Rain-Storm god (Susa-no-wo) from that which filled his nostrils.

Many are the stories told of Amaterasu and Susa-no-wo, between whom the rule of the universe was divided after the disappearance of the primeval divine couple.[1] Curiously the Moon-god never plays any prominent part. ' The Sun-goddess, or the Heaven-illumining Lady, was bright and beautiful in features, unrivalled in dignity, benign, honest and meek in temper. She ruled wisely and brilliantly the realm assigned to her, giving light and life to all, and she also protected the rice-fields by constructing irrigation canals. Besides, she is represented as the organizer of religious rites, especially those in observance of the rules of purity. In short she was the presiding deity of peace and order, of agriculture and food supply. Herein we can detect a representation of the rôle of womanhood played in the early rise of peaceful social order and agricultural pursuits. On the other hand, her brother, the Swift-Impetuous, was wild, arrogant and disobedient. He cried in wild fury, disregarding all his duties, and raged in the air between heaven and earth. The details of his atrocities against his sister in heaven remind us strongly of storm-gods in other mythologies.'[2]

One story told of the relations of Amaterasu and Susa-no-wo is obviously a mythological account of a

---

[1] We are told nothing definite about the end of Izanagi, except that he finally hid himself or is abiding in the Solar Palace of Youth.
[2] Anesaki, p. 27.

solar eclipse. It represents the reverence paid to the
sun as the source of life by a primitive, agricultural
people and throws some light upon their religious
practices at the time of a solar eclipse. The Rain-
Storm god, we are told, destroyed the rice-fields
cultivated by his sister and greatly distressed her
by certain wanton acts. He flung dung into the
sacred hall in which she was celebrating the feast of
first-fruits and threw the carcase of a piebald colt,
which had been flayed backwards, beginning at the
tail, into the room where the goddess was weaving
garments for the deities. Amaterasu was so outraged
by this misconduct that she shut herself up in the
Rock Cave of heaven and left the celestial and terrestrial world in darkness. Dire results followed. ' The
voices of evil deities were like unto the flies in the fifth
moon as they swarmed, and a myriad portents of woe
arose.' ' The gods, in consternation, held an assembly
in the dry bed of the River of Heaven (the Milky Way)
to devise means for inducing her to emerge from the
cave, and a number of expedients were adopted which
were evidently borrowed from the ritual of the time
when the myth became current. The deities who were
specially concerned with this duty are obvious counterparts of the actual officials of the Mikado's court and
included a prayer-reciter, an offering provider, a
mirror-maker, a jewel-maker, a diviner, with—according to some accounts—many others. All this is most
convenient to the genealogists of later times.'[1] At
length Amaterasu reappears. She had heard the loud
laughter evoked from the gods by the lewd dance of
a certain goddess ; and, moved by curiosity to know
the cause of the laughter, she opened the door of her

[1] Aston, S.A.R.J., pp. 25f.

cave a little, whereupon the god Stronghand seized her and prevented her from retreating into the cave again.[1] When the light and order had been restored by the reappearance of the goddess, all the assembly burst into shouts of joy. The council of the gods commanded Susa-no-wo's beard to be cut off and his toe-nails and finger-nails to be pulled out. He was also to be fined a thousand tables of offerings and banished from heaven.

Susa-no-wo next ' appears in a totally new character as the Perseus of a Japanese Andromeda, whom he rescues from a huge serpent, having first intoxicated the monster. Of course, they are married and have numerous children. Her name, Inada-hime (rice-land-lady), is probably not without significance as that of the wife of a Rain-Storm god.'[2]

A curious point worth noticing is that, though Amaterasu and Susa-no-wo are represented as being in perpetual conflict, each is said to have given birth to children by the ' inspiration' of the other. On one occasion, according to the *Kojiki*, they exchanged their treasures. She took his sword and he took her jewels. Five male and three female children were born when each crunched in the mouth and spat out the fragments of the sword and jewels worn by the other. At another time brother and sister gave birth to another eight children by a mutual oath of miraculous virtue. Such stories were, no doubt, designed to express in mythological fashion the truth that the sun and the rain co-operate in the production of crops. The *Kojiki* traces back to these

[1] In Aston, S.W.G. (pp. 98) there is a reproduction of an interesting Japanese picture showing Stronghand grasping the Sun-goddess through the half-open door of the cave.
[2] Aston, S.A.R.J., p. 26.

children the origin of some of the noble families of Japan.

One of Susa-no-wo's many children was Ohonamochi (Great-Name-Possessor). As his various names show, he was an earth-god who is to this day worshipped in the province of Idzuma. His adventures are related at great length in the *Kojiki*. By various mothers he had many children, among whom were the Harvest-god and the Food-goddess. In the meantime, the Sun-goddess had decided to dispossess Ohonamochi in order that her grandson, Ninigi, might reign over Japan. Ohonamochi gave way to the request of Amaterasu and accordingly Ninigi came down to earth with a great retinue of attendants. He married a Mountain-god's daughter by whom he had three children. His second son, Hohodemi, married the Sea-god's daughter and one of their grandchildren was Jimmu Tenno, who is usually reckoned as the first emperor of Japan and founder of the Imperial Dynasty. He is said to have conquered Yamato, the central part of Japan, in 667 B.C. and to have established his capital there in 660 B.C.

The aim of the foregoing myth, which is found both in the *Kojiki* and the *Nihongi*, is to teach the divine origin of the Emperors of Japan and to claim for them direct descent in unbroken line from the Sun-goddess, by whom the first Emperor Jimmu was invested with the Three Insignia of the Throne, the Divine Mirror, Sword and Jewel.[1] The *Nihongi* more than once expressly claims that the Mikado ' rules the world as God incarnate,' and implies that the dynasty will last

[1] The mirror is deposited in the sanctuary of the Sun-goddess in Isé ; the sword in another sanctuary ; the jewel is the personal possession of the Emperor. cf. Anesaki, p. 38 and note.

for ever. Taken literally, the myth would mean that Japan has never had any other ruler than the Mikado, who, from the beginning, has reigned over all the land as an incarnate deity. Such a view is quite unhistorical. Indeed, the *Nihongi* itself contains ample evidence to show that the actual sovereignty of the Emperor was built up only gradually and after years of strenuous fighting against independent tribes and chieftains. The myth of the Emperor's descent from the Sun-goddess obviously took shape at a time when the Japanese were beginning to recognize themselves as a united people under the rule of one emperor as their head.

During the nineteenth century, Japanese scholars became increasingly aware of the fact that the myths of the *Kojiki* and *Nihongi* were self-contradictory. They felt keenly the need of giving a new interpretation to the ancient myths and, therefore, advanced the hypothesis that they are capable of both a literal and an allegorical interpretation. They explained away all the difficulties which present themselves to a modern mind by giving them a figurative interpretation. Thus, the story in the *Nihongi* of how a certain goddess transformed herself into a crocodile or dragon when about to be delivered of a child, was taken as an allegorical expression of her labour pains in childbirth. One of the champions of the allegorical method of interpretation was Kamo-Norikiyo (d. 1861). By this device he made a valiant attempt to derive from the myths moral teaching which would satisfy the advanced ethical consciousness of his time. Thus ' he interpreted figuratively the passage of the *Nihongi* according to which the Emperor Jimmu met with almost insurmountable difficulties in leading his troops on his expedition to the eastern district.'[1] The Emperor's foes, he maintained, were not ordinary foes of flesh and blood but his invisible, impalpable inward foes. Other writers found a figurative interpretation for the Three Insignia of the Throne. 'The Mirror,' said such an one, 'reflects from its bright surface every object as it really is, irrespective of goodness or badness, beauty or the reverse. This is the very nature of the Mirror, which faithfully symbolizes truthfulness, one of the cardinal virtues. The Jewel signifies softheartedness and obedience, so that it becomes a symbol of benevolence. The Sword represents the virtue of strong decision, *i.e.* wisdom. Without the combined strength of these three fundamental virtues peace in the realm cannot be expected.'[2]

Later, the reliability of the *Kojiki* and *Nihongi* as historical records was rejected on critical grounds. The first Japanese scholar to do this was Professor Kumé of the Imperial University of Tokyo. He was deprived of his Chair for thus impugning the orthodox Shinto belief. To-day, however, some Japanese scholars, in seeking to discredit the myths of Shinto, go so far as to speak of them as 'olden time jokes for the children's amusement.'[3]

---

[1] Kato, p. 147.   [2] Cited by Kato, pp. 149f.
[3] See Kato, p. 149. The student who wishes to go into further detail should consult the article by Revon on 'Cosmogony and Cosmology (Japanese)' in the E.R.E. IV, pp. 162-7. It cites many parallels from other nations.

CHAPTER IV

THE PANTHEON

ACCORDING to the Japanese, who call their country 'The Land of the Gods,' the Shinto pantheon contains no fewer than eight or eighty myriads of gods, which is their way of saying that the gods are so many that it is impossible to enumerate them individually. Not only was nature portioned out among the deities but all human affairs were placed under the care of special tutelary deities. 'These presided over the various crafts and callings, and even over inanimate tools and utensils. The naïve Japanese mind was continually busy constructing a petty deity for everything that met the eye.'[1] Hence 'the number of effective deities fluctuates greatly. Oblivion disposes of many. The identification of distinct deities is another cause of depletion in their ranks . . . On the other hand their numbers are recruited from time to time by new gods produced by various processes.'[2]

The classification of so varied and fluctuating a pantheon is no easy matter. We cannot do better than follow here the classification proposed by Aston. He first divides the pantheon into Nature-gods and Man-gods, the first being the result of personification, the second of deification. In each of these two classes he makes three sub-divisions according as the deity

---

[1] Krause in Clemen's *Religions of the World*, p. 256. cf. the quotation from Nitobe above, p. 18
[2] Aston, S.W.G., p. 66f.

represents an individual object, a class or an abstract quality.[1]

Aston's classification may be shown thus :

I.   NATURE-GODS :
   (a) Gods representing an individual object, e.g. the Sun-goddess.
   (b) Gods representing a class, e.g. Kukuchi, the god of Trees.
   (c) Gods representing an abstract quality in nature, e.g. Musubi, the god of Growth.

II.   MAN-GODS :
   (a) Gods representing a deified individual, e.g. Temmangu is a deified statesman.
   (b) Gods representing a clan or family, e.g. Koyane, the god of the Nakatomi clan or family.
   (c) Gods representing a personified human quality, e.g. Taji-kara-no-wo (Hand-Strength-Male or Stronghand).

Something may now be said about the principal gods of the pantheon. It is important to bear in mind that they have not all been regarded as of equal importance, nor have they all been worshipped by the mass of the people. Since Shinto is essentially a form of nature-worship, the nature-gods are the most important members of the pantheon.

The first place among the nature-deities is held by Amaterasu, the Sun-goddess. She ' was originally conceived as the sun itself, soul and body, a living spirit united to its brilliant covering.'[2] Much Shinto mythology is concerned with her birth and exploits. As the Ruler of Heaven she is unrivalled in dignity. As the Sun-goddess, Amaterasu plays an important

1 Aston, S.A.R.J., p. 8ff.   2 Revon in E.R.E., IX, p. 235.

part in the agricultural rites of the Japanese ; as the progenitrix of the divine Mikado she also plays an important political rôle. Thus at one and the same time she embodies the life-giving power of an agricultural deity and the attribute of wise rulership. As she is easily worshippped, she has many shrines, but the chief centre of her cult is at Isé, which is the most sacred spot in all Japan.[1] ' Even to-day the Japanese always worship the sun as a living deity, to whom they render a direct positive cult, from the artizan, who, from the depths of his dark shop, turns towards the brightness of the dawn, claps his hands, and piously recites his prayer to the goddess, to the pilgrim who on the summit of Fujiyama prostrates himself dazzled before the first golden rays of the sun and worships it leaning his forehead on the rocks.'[2]

The Moon-god (Tsuki-yomi) is masculine. His dominion is that of the night, as his sister's is that of the day. He is worshipped at a few shrines but occupies quite an inferior place in the pantheon compared with that held by his sister, Amaterasu. He has not her conquering brilliance. In Japanese moon-worship at the present day, ' the æsthetic sentiment is more predominant than the religious. But the moon none the less receives, with the homage due to its beauty, the offerings reserved for the divine powers ; the people who go to witness its superb rising at certain times and certain favourite places proceed from admiration to prayer ; the enchantment of the eyes is completed by the adoration of the heart.'[3]

The star-gods have never occupied any significant

[1] For an account of her temple and cultus, see below, pp. 54f.
[2] Revon in E.R.E., IX, p. 235. See also, Griffis, pp. 87f.
[3] Revon, in E.R.E., IX, p. 235.

position in ancient Shinto, though there are indications that the stars were once deified.

Susa-no-wo, the Rain-Storm god, is a personification of the rain-storm. He dwells in the air as the gods just mentioned dwell in the sky. His deification is due, no doubt, to the fact that Japan is a land in which storms are rightly dreaded. His full title is 'the august impetuous male, swift and brave.' Something has already been said about his place in Shinto mythology, which represents him as weeping, crying and groaning continually ; as leaving his sea-dwelling and shaking the whole country.

Other nature-deities, whose abode is the air, are the Wind-gods, the Rain-gods, the Thunder-god and the Fire-god. The Wind-gods are gentle and their beneficent activities are contrasted with the wicked furies of Susa-no-wo. They represent the normal wind which blows 'with long slow breaths' and sweeps away the morning mists. They are always kindly, provided men do not irritate them by their neglect. As Revon points out[1] their deification can be easily understood in a country of mountains where morning mists are common. And if the light breezes purify the air by sweeping away mists, autumn squalls may ruin the hopes of the cultivators. Moreover, the winds were sure to have a divine function ascribed to them in a land whose climate is governed by the monsoons. The Rain-gods are not very prominent, though Japan has an abundant rain-fall. The Thunder-god is feared even to this day. ' The common people are afraid of thunder, and even the educated show some uneasiness when its voice rumbles like a mysterious warning from heaven.'[2] The mythological account of the birth of

[1] E.R.E., IX, p. 236.   [2] Revon, in E.R.E., IX, p. 236.

the Fire-god has already been mentioned. His
evolution and character are readily explained if we
bear in mind the frail character of Japanese houses.
'In such a country fire was an enemy. Its former
benefits, its daily uses, were forgotten; only its
terrifying frolics were seen. If the Fire-god was
worshipped, it was not because he was admired or
loved, as among other races, but because he was feared.
The people tried to exorcize him. He is regarded in
the same way to-day, especially as a force of nature
against which one must make sure of safe-guarding
one's house by amulets, &c.; he is not so much a god
of fire, in the broad sense of the word, as a god of
conflagration.'[1]

The nature deities who inhabit the earth are the
Sea-gods, the Land-gods, the Mountain-gods, and the
River-gods. The supreme sea-god is Oho-wata-tsu-mi,
'the great god of the ocean.' He has a wonderful
palace hidden in the depths of the sea. Since their
land is an archipelago, 'the sea which envelops it is
the first thing that attracts attention, and it is very
probable that it held this dominant place in the
imagination of the primitive Japanese.'[2] There are
also secondary sea-gods—gods of the middle of the sea,
gods of the bottom of the sea, gods of the surface of
the sea, gods of the river-mouths, gods of froth and
foam. 'The whole sea therefore lives, animated,
spiritualized, deified, and becomes transformed into a
crowd of gods.'[3] In Shinto the earth is deified in
various forms and an earth-god is usually propitiated
before a new building is erected or new land brought
under cultivation. 'All these land-gods are very

---

[1] Revon, *op. cit. loc. cit.*   [2] Ibid.
[3] Revon, in E.R.E., IX, p. 237.

vague, and too abstract to make a clear impression on the mind ; the religious imagination requires individual concrete visions. This explains why the mountain-gods appear in the first rank of the gods of the earth. Nothing could be more natural in a country dominated by its orographic system, a country whose general appearance recalls that of Switzerland, whose whole beauty depends on the continual play of mountains and valleys, dark gorges descending from the heights and graceful hillocks undulating towards the plains, stern summits and smiling landscapes. All these raised portions of the earth were reflected in the depths of the primitive soul, which made them objects of general deification.'[1] Mount Fujiyama is the most venerated among the sacred mountains of Japan. The *Manyo-shiu* speaks of it as ' a wondrous deity . . . and a guardian of the land of Japan.'[2] The mountain-deities are propitiated before the trees on their sides are cut down. The River-gods of Shinto are not important. ' The reason is that the hydrographic system of the country is as modest as its orographic system is preponderating.'[3]

One nature deity has his dwelling underground. He is the Earthquake-god. ' He receives very sincere worship through terror, because his dreadful convulsions, which are worse than flood, plague, or fire, are the only scourge against which man cannot fight.'[4]

The magnificence of the flora of Japan led to the deification of plants as well as trees. Animals were also deified and classed as *kami* (superior beings), because, no doubt, primitive man feared some of them

[1] Revon, in E.R.E., IX, p. 237.   [2] Cited by Kato, p. 11.
[3] Revon, in E.R.E., IX, p. 237.   [4] Ibid.

and admired the power and agility of others. The worship of the serpent is wide-spread in Shinto, and ' is explained both by the alarming appearance of that creeping, glazed, often dangerous animal and by its abundance in the thickets of the primitive country.'[1] Birds are deified because they ' share in a way the superior nature of the sky ; man envies their wings and is surprised at their mysterious language ; he admires those creatures so swift of flight, at one moment mounting to the abode of the gods and the next settling down beside other creatures and chirping as if telling them strange secrets. Thus in the myths their essential function is that of divine messengers, and nearly always, when a person sees them appearing, he guesses that they are bringing news or a command from heaven.'[2] Even fishes and insects did not escape the tendency to deification. ' In a word, whether these animals are the object of great adoration or only of slight respect, it is always because of the same old naturism which gives a spirit to each one, humanizes and deifies animals as well as plants, and with the same breath raises the humble lives of the organic universe and the phenomena of the material world to the higher regions.'[3]

Among the nature-deities which represent an abstract quality in nature Aston places the Divine Couple, Izanagi and Izanami. ' I have little doubt,' he says, ' that these deities were suggested by the Yin and Yang, or male and female principles of Chinese philosophy. They were probably introduced into Japanese myth in order to account for the existence of the Sun-goddess and other deities, and to link them

---

[1] Revon, in E.R.E., IX, p. 238. [2] Ibid.
[3] Ibid., p. 239.

together by a common parentage . . . They are not important in ritual.'[1]

Musubi, the god of Growth, belongs to the same category. His worship once held a prominent place in the Imperial Palace but it is now neglected.

It is difficult to know in which of Aston's categories to place the Food-goddess. She is sometimes called Toyo-uke-bime. Another of her names is Uke-mochi (' Food-possessor ') ; but she has many aliases. There is a real sense in which she is a nature deity, though there is no one compartment of nature in which she is domiciled. Yet she has a definite function in the physical world. She is not only a goddess of cereals, but also provides fish and game, and, indeed, clothing and housing for men. She, therefore, surpasses the flora and fauna and hovers over the whole of nature. At the same time her functions keep her among the spirits of material phenomena.[2] Her worship goes back to most ancient times. She is invoked by the peasantry to give them good crops. She is, indeed, the most important member of the Shinto pantheon, after the Sun-goddess. In some of the greatest shrines she receives the main honours and is worshipped even in Isé, which is specially sacred to the Sun-goddess.

The Sahe-no-kami, or phallic deities, are best included among the gods representing an abstract quality in nature, though Aston does not include them in this category. The early Japanese, in common with many other primitive peoples, viewed the mystery of the propagation of life with religious awe as one of the many manifestations of the divine. Thus

[1] Aston, S.A.R.J., p. 47.
[2] cf. Revon, in E.R.E., IX, p. 239.

phallic emblems were generally worshipped in ancient times. The phallic cult of ancient Shinto really forms ' an integral part of its essential naturism ; and, as it considers paternity the highest mission of the gods, it worships in all simplicity, the instrument of this supreme function.'[1] The close connexion of this worship with agricultural Shinto rites [2] shows that the underlying idea was that of the promotion of fertility.[3] No doubt the spread of Buddhist philosophy and Confucian ethics made it difficult for enlightened minds to continue this crude form of worship and the phallus thus lost its primary significance and came to be used in the main as a prophylactic appliance for warding off epidemic and contagious diseases. ' The apotropaic virtue of this symbol . . . is due to the association of virility with manly strength, power to overcome invisible foes as well as visible, and to protect those in need of help.'[4] Since 1868, most phallic emblems have been removed from public view by order of the Government, but Dr. Kato says that even now in secluded parts of the land phallic worship is continued. He mentions various *kami*, each of which ' is a veritable Japanese Priapos,' and seems to imply that rites of an obscene, orgiastic character are still continued at various shrines when spring-time festivals are observed.[5]

Turning now to deified individual men, we notice that national heroes, rulers, warriors, inventors and other benefactors, who had earned the gratitude of the nation, were always more or less deified and

[1] Revon, in E.R.E., IX, p. 239.   [2] See Kato, p. 3of.
[3] This is denied by Moore in his *History of Religions*, Vol. I, p. 108.   [4] Moore, *op. cit. loc. cit.*
[5] Kato, pp. 3of.   cf. Aston, S.W.G., p. 198, and E.R.E., IX, p. 239.

worship was offered to them. This deification of human beings ' is peculiarly easy in Japan because the language employs the same word, *kami* (literally, " high, exalted " in both physical and figurative senses), for the " superiors," whom we should call gods (cf. Latin *superi*), and for human superiors, living or dead.'[1] As examples of this type of deity, we may mention the war-god, Hachiman, whom tradition, probably wrongly, identifies with the Emperor Ojin. His cult has, however, been greatly influenced by Buddhism.[2] Temmangu is the god of Learning and Calligraphy, who is much worshipped by school-boys and their teachers. The circumstances, in which this deification of an individual human being was effected, are known to us. Temmangu is the name given to a certain Sugawara-no-Michizane when he was raised to divine rank. He was born in A.D. 845 and died in 903. His great learning gained him high rank in the government and enabled him to establish a system of national education, which gained for him the gratitude of the people. Owing to the machinations of a rival, he was banished and died in exile. The great calamities which followed his exile led to his deification and the establishment of shrines in his honour. In this case Chinese influences may be suspected. It is not impossible that his cult was suggested by the honours paid by the Chinese to Confucius.

Some have thought that the elevation of individual men to the rank of deities would never have occurred in Shinto had it not been stimulated by Chinese influences. But a careful examination of the evidence seems to show that there was anthropolatry in Shinto from

---

[1] Moore, *History of Religions*, Vol. I, pp. 95f.
[2] See further Aston, S.W.G., pp. 178f.

the very first.[1] It is present in the mythology of the *Kojiki* which mentions among others the deification of the man who first invented the blacksmith's art. Indeed, the development of anthropolatry was almost inevitable. ' Just as the ancient Japanese used to worship the forces of nature, so they bowed before human powers. Out of the admiration which they felt for certain visible and living men grew the more abstract worship of the same men after their death.'[2] According to Revon the worship of hero-gods still exists in Japan in a profoundly living form.[3]

The most conspicuous example of the deification of an individual man is, of course, the cult of the Mikado, a feature of Shinto which has received great emphasis in modern times since the restoration of the Emperor to power in 1868. Aston is inclined to think that the honours paid to living and dead Mikados are of doubtful religious quality. Speaking of the earliest days, he says ' their godship was more titular than real. It was much on a par with that of the Pope and the Emperor who, in the Middle Ages, were called " Deus in terris." No miraculous powers were claimed for them beyond a vague general authority over the minor gods of Japan . . . They had no shrines, and no rituals in their honour are preserved in the *Yengi-shiki*.'[4] Aston, however, concedes that in later times there was a definite cult of deceased Mikados who were prayed to for rain, to stay curses, to restore the health of the living Mikado, &c. At the present time the worship of all the dynasty is solemnly celebrated in the Imperial Palace.

---

[1] As Kato (p. 80, cf. p. 51) claims.
[2] Revon, in E.R.E., VI, p. 662.   [3] E.R.E., VI, p. 663.
[4] Aston, S.A.R.J., pp. 10f.

That the living Mikado is entitled to divine reverence has already been shown in our treatment of the myth dealing with his descent from the Sun-goddess. In his decree he may describe himself as 'Manifest Deity.' His person is spoken of in the Constitution of 1889 as 'sacred and inviolable.' The famous Imperial Rescript on Education of 1890 speaks of his throne as 'coeval with heaven and earth, infallible for all ages.' It is noteworthy that, though the shoguns did not hesitate to rob the Emperor of all political power for many centuries prior to 1868, none of them ever dared to put himself in the Emperor's place or to violate his person. It was blasphemy even to speak of deposing an emperor, however unworthy he might be. Dr. Kato does not hesitate to say with an obvious touch of pride that 'Shinto, as a theanthropic religion, has culminated in Mikadoism or the worship of the Mikado or Japanese Emperor, as a divinity, during his lifetime as well as after his death.'[1] Most modern scholars would agree that once the Emperor had become undisputed master of the land and the high priest of the nation, his deification would follow. If lesser benefactors, conquerors and civilizers were worthy of deification, his claim to rank as a deity was obvious. The Shinto tendency to deify the nation's heroes simply came to a climax in the divine honours paid to him.

Concerning the gods of Classes of Men, which hold a fairly prominent position in early Shinto, we cannot do better than quote Aston. 'In imitation of the Mikados, who selected the Sun-goddess as their ancestral deity, the hereditary corporations or clans by whom in ancient times the Government of Japan,

[1] *Op. cit.*, p. 206.

central and local, was carried on, chose for themselves, or perhaps invented, nature-deities, or their children or ministers, as their patron-gods, to whom special worship was paid . . . These pseudo-ancestral deities were called Uji-gami, that is to say, "surname deities." In later times the Uji-gami ceased to be the patron-gods of particular families and became simply the local deities of the district where one was born. Children are presented to the Uji-gami shortly after birth, and other important events, such as a change of residence, are announced to him.'[1]

The gods of Human Qualities are not very numerous as the Japanese were not very apt at personifying abstract human qualities. We do not find in the Shinto pantheon such conceptions as Age, Youth, Love, Fear, Patience, Hope, and Charity. The deity Strong-hand is the best example of this class but he is little worshipped and figures only as a poetical adjunct to the myth of the Sun-goddess's retirement to a cave. Aston places the phallic deities in this category, but we have thought it more in accord with recent scholarship to include them among the nature deities.

From what has been said, it will be seen that the Nature-gods of Shinto are the actual material objects or phenomena of nature regarded as living beings. In many cases, though not in all, personification is carried to the lengths of the crudest anthropomorphism. The gods act and speak in a very unspiritual fashion exactly like the primitive Japanese. Their doings are reported with a directness and naïveté which is, to say the least, surprising. 'They are born, wed, beget

1 Aston, S.A.R.J., pp. 9f. See also p. 52 and cf. Anesaki, p. 34, and Aston, S.W.G., pp. 183ff.

children, vomit, bathe, become sick, vexed, jealous, weep, curse, kill, destroy, die, are buried in a certain place, and subsequently may be raised in rank by the Emperor of Japan . . . No human being in Japan now would be allowed to do with impunity what the god Susa-no-wo is reported to have done, nor what the other deities did to him in punishment of his offence.'[1] Of Izanagi and Izanami it is not too much to say that they live in a state of copulatory ferment.[2] This explains why the translator of the *Kojiki* resorts to Latin in a number of passages in order to veil their obscenity. Amaterasu is, of course, a much loftier figure but even she is anthropomorphically conceived as weaving, wearing armour and sowing seed, and hiding in a cave.

Nevertheless there are indications of higher ideas. 'Some of the gods are represented as having *mitama* (august jewels or souls) which reside invisibly in their temples and are the means of communication between heaven and earth.'[3] Thus it is said that it is not the Sun-goddess herself who inhabits her shrine at Isé but her *mitama*, which is likened by Aston to the *shekinah* of the Jews. The Earth-deity is said to have had a *mitama* (double) which appeared to him in a divine radiance illuminating the sea.[4] 'The *mitama* is represented in the shrine by a concrete object termed the *shintai* or "god-body." It may be a mirror, a sword, a tablet with the god's name, a pillow, a spear,

---

[1] Hume, *The World's Living Religions*, p. 152.

[2] They beget the seas, rivers, mountains, Japan itself, and even trees and herbs just as a human pair beget children. Dr. Kato (*op. cit.*, p. 85) naïvely claims that this shows that in Shinto gods and men alike are subject to natural law and cannot escape it.　　　　　　　　　　　　　　　[3] Aston, S.A.R.J., p. 14

[4] See Aston, S.W.G., pp. 26f., and the picture of the deity and his double on pp. 28f.

&c. A round stone, which is cheap and durable, is a very common *shintai*. The god is sometimes represented as attaching himself to the *shintai*, and may be even considered identical with it by the ignorant. The *mitama* and *shintai* are frequently confounded.'[1]

Shinto is incurably polytheistic. The impulse which led to the deification of one natural object led in time to the deification of countless others. Moreover, the early Japanese had not sufficient scientific knowledge or philosophical acumen to enable them to grasp the unity of nature and to posit behind it one great living spirit. Theirs was the crude philosophy of animism and they never advanced from it to anything like pantheism.

Realizing the defects of what he calls Shinto's ' downright polytheism,' Dr. Kato has recently tried to show that ' we can discern the germ of naturalistic pantheism in Shinto even in its oldest documents.'[2] He points to passages in which natural objects are said to have originated from portions of the body of one and the same god. He cites the following passage from the *Nihongi* which records how animals and plants sprang from the corpse of the Food-goddess. ' On the crown of her head there had been produced the ox and the horse ; on the top of her forehead there had been produced millet ; over her eyebrows there had been produced the silkworm ; within her eyes there had been produced panic ; in her belly there had been produced rice ; in her genitals there had been produced wheat, large beans and small beans.' He also points out, that according to the same authority the cryptomeria trees were produced when Susa-no-wo plucked out his beard and scattered it about ; that the

[1] Aston, S.A.R.J., p. 16.   [2] Kato, pp. 138f.

eye-brows of the same god became camphor trees ;
that Susa-no-wo, Amaterasu and Tsuki-yomi sprang
respectively from the nose and the left and right eyes
of Izanagi. Dr. Kato's argument may be good Shinto
apologetic but it is much too naïve to commend itself
to trained anthropologists, who would regard it as a
complete misreading of the available evidence.

Encouraged by Andrew Lang's theory that a
primitive monotheism can be found among some
peoples living in low cultural lands, Dr. Kato has
also tried to find in the old Japanese pantheon a god
who may be regarded as the deity of a primitive
Japanese monotheism. He finds him in one of the
three deities who are said to have sprung out of the
primeval chaos and then disappeared.[1] This deity
rejoices in the name of ' Divine Lord of the Very
Centre of Heaven.' Dr. Kato acclaims him as the
god of the ' primitive monotheism indigenous to the
soil of Japan.'[2] Again, it must be said that Dr. Kato
forces the evidence to yield a conclusion it will not
sustain. His theory is nothing like so probable as
that mentioned above.[3] Aston does not exaggerate
when he says that ' monotheism was an impossibility
in ancient Japan.'[4]

It is nevertheless possible to trace certain tendencies
towards monotheism, especially in connexion with
the cult of the Sun-goddess. At the dawn of the
historical period there was a marked tendency for her
cult to preponderate over that of the local deities and
miscellaneous spirits for the following reasons. As
the power of the ruling family grew and national unity
took shape, some of the subjugated clans would bring

[1] See p. 23 above.　　[2] Kato, p. 66.
[3] Supra, p. 24.　　[4] Aston, S.W.G., p. 68.

their clan deities under the hegemony of the Sun-goddess, who was the divine progenitrix of the ruling house. ' Thus the growth of national unity was a political and religious issue, and was symbolized in a central seat of worship dedicated to the Great Deity, which was established at Isé on the sea-coast facing the east. Even to-day Isé remains the holy of holies of the Shinto cult.'[1] The rapid transition of the Japanese from a life of hunting and fishing to that of agriculture, and especially to the cultivation of rice, worked in the same direction, for the Sun-goddess was naturally adored as the protectress of agriculture, as the Harvest Festival and the Festival of First Fruits show. In short, the general tendency to regard the Sun-goddess as a general Providence at the expense of other deities necessarily involved a step in the direction of monotheism.

For two reasons, however, this monotheism was never actually established. (1) The tribal cults were never suppressed by the central government. Nor could they be in a land broken up by hills and inlets of the sea, which separated group from group and bound each of them into a compact community. Thus any tendency to monotheism was counteracted by the tendency to polytheism created by the tenacity of the local and tribal cults. (2) The theistic development of Shinto was crippled at a comparatively early date by the intrusion of Buddhism into Japan. Later forms of Shinto moved in the direction of assimilation to Buddhism rather than towards the elevation of one of the indigenous deities into a supreme and sole deity.[2]

[1] Anesaki, p. 32.
[2] On the subject of conceptions which pave the way to monotheism see further Aston, S.W.G., pp. 68ff., and p. 349.

4

CHAPTER V

WORSHIP, PRIESTHOOD AND RITUAL

In the earliest times the dwelling-place of a god in Japan was not a building but a sacred plot of ground enclosed by a stone wall. Shinto temples were first erected about the beginning of the Christian era. They have always been, and are to this day, simple constructions of unpainted wood. A few straight pillars are fixed in the earth and covered with a roof which is generally of bark. The tiled roof betrays the influences of Buddhism. In Anesaki and Kato there are excellent pictures of Shinto temples which the student would do well to examine. The shrine is obviously a miniature Japanese dwelling-house. Shinto shrines, which are found in great numbers throughout Japan, are usually built in wooded places, generally under the shade of a cryptomeria grove, and thus the atmosphere of primitive nature-worship is preserved. Shintoists 'have never built a stone cathedral; their holy places were temples of nature wherein a group of huge trees rivalled a Gothic tower.' ' The situation of the sombre-looking shrine among old trees in the dim light of wooded places contributes very much to the austerity of the sanctuary. This sequestered solemnity is characterized by such words as " god-like," " divinely serene." '[1]

Every Shinto shrine has a *tori-i* [2] standing at its

[1] Anesaki, p. 41.
[2] The meaning of *tori-i* is still under discussion. Some take it to be a bird-perch.

entrance. ' It is a simple structure, either in wood or stone, made up of two quadrangular beams laid horizontally above the head and supported by two round columns. This is the portal, and it stands at the entrance to a long avenue of trees, and at intervals, as well as in front of the shrine . . . Thus, the portals, the avenue, and the woods, together with the shrine and various sacred symbols, make up a Shinto sanctuary.'[1]

The shrine itself generally has two rooms. In front there is an open prayer-hall for the worshippers and behind a sanctuary which only the priest may enter and which contains the emblem of the deity. There is always a laver in the court-yard for use in ceremonial ablutions and usually a stage used in connexion with the religious dances and dramatic performances mentioned below. The greater temples have several courts and a number of buildings, one of which is used for the reception of votive offerings, such as swords and the tablets with a horse drawn on them (*ema*) which are the modern substitute for the ancient horse-offering. No temple is complete without its *gohei*, which Professor Anesaki describes as ' a small pole of wood or bamboo in which is inserted a piece of paper or cloth, so cut that the two parts hang down on the two sides of the pole and each part looks plaited.'[2] The *gohei* is a substitute for the offering of fibre cloth which in ancient times was offered to the gods on the bough of a tree. To-day the *gohei* is little more than a symbol of sanctity or divinity. The whole of the sacred precincts is enclosed by a wooden fence. Within the precincts every specially sacred object or place has hung before it a thick rope

[1] Anesaki, p. 42 and Plate I.B.   [2] Anesaki, p. 42.

of twisted rice-straw upon which pieces of paper are
hung. (See illustration in Kato of the Oratory of
the main shrine of Izumo.) It is called the demarcation
rope (*shime-naha*) and is supposed to keep off evil
influences.[1]

There are no visible objects of worship, but within
the shrine is the emblem or symbol of the deity. The
concrete object thus used is called the *shintai*, ' god-
body,' or *mitama-shiro*, ' spirit-substitute.' It is
generally a mirror but in some shrines a sword, a
spear, a pillow or even a round stone is found. The
ignorant may regard the god and the *shintai* as
identical, but Shinto theologians would express themselves more carefully and speak of it as a symbolic
representation of the deity, and so avoid the least
suggestion of idolatry. The mirror in the famous
shrine at Isé is said by the *Kojiki* and the *Nihongi*
to be the very one given by the Sun-goddess to her
grandson when she sent him to subdue the land.
' Regard it as my august spirit,' and worship it as if
thou wert worshipping in my presence,' she said to
him, according to the *Kojiki*. The *Kojiki* gives the
mythical story of how it was forged and the *Nihongi*
tells how the emperor came to part with it and how it
finally came to rest at the temple of the Sun-goddess
in Isé. It was by a natural extension of the influence
of so important a shrine as that of Amaterasu in Isé
that many Shinto deities came to be represented by
a mirror, which is exhibited in all shrines except hers.

[1] The student may further consult the articles *Architecture*
(*Shinto*) and *Art* (*Shinto*) in E.R.E.

[2] It is a common idea among primitive people that mysterious
relations may exist between a mirror and a soul. Revon speaks
of the mirror at Isé as ' a primitive talisman which afterwards
became the greatest national fetish.' E.R.E., XII, 803.

The mirror of Amaterasu in Isé is never seen by human eyes—not even those of the priests. It is 'enclosed in a brocade bag, which is never opened ; when the old material shows signs of giving way, the whole is put into a new bag : so that to-day the mirror is enfolded in several layers of silk. Thus protected, it is in addition enclosed in a box, provided with eight handles, placed on a slightly raised stand, and covered with a piece of white silk. Lastly, above all this there is a sort of cage of white wood, with ornaments of pure gold, itself enveloped in a rough silk curtain, which reaches to the ground on every side. These coverings of the box are all that the people are allowed to see on the festivals on which the sanctuary is opened. Viscount Mori, the Minister of Public Instruction, who dared to raise a corner of the outer curtain of the sanctuary at Isé, was soon after, on the very day on which the new constitution of Japan was proclaimed in 1889, assassinated by a fanatic Shintoist, whose tomb became a place of pilgrimage.'[1]

The daily worship performed at Shinto shrines is not, as a rule, congregational but individual. The worshipper brings his offerings and bows twice both before and after making them. 'Kneeling is also known, but is less usual . . . Clapping hands was in ancient Japan a general token of respect, now confined to religious worship. Sometimes a silent hand-clapping is prescribed in the rituals.'[2] 'The priests serving in these ceremonies glide in and out of the sanctuary with quiet footsteps, silence being strictly observed . . . In this way Shinto ceremonial is peculiarly pure and solemnly quiet. These features give to it an

[1] E.R.E., XII, p. 803.   [2] Aston, S.A.R.J., p. 59.

archaic sobriety, and Shintoists are proud of this as an evidence of its direct derivation from the celestial world. But as a matter of fact the quiet feature of the official rites was chiefly derived from the solemnity of court ceremonies.'[1]

There are, however, occasions on which Shinto temples present a more joyous spectacle. Dances, with songs and musical accompaniment, and also dramatic representations are given in a separate building, in the presence of the worshippers. In this way the old folk-tales are disseminated among the people, though no attempt is made by the priests to give the people any systematic instruction in the legends or in the ritual. These pantomimic dances, which are called *kagura*, have become, as in other countries, the parent of the secular drama.

By far the most famous of all Shinto shrines is that at Isé. It is dedicated to Amaterasu, the Sun-goddess, and, as has been already said, contains within its sanctuary the mirror given by the goddess to her divine offspring, the Mikado. It is the most sacred spot in all Japan. Its antiquity is vouched for by the fact that the *Kojiki* and the *Nihongi* contain references to it and to the manner in which its cultus is carried on. The shrine is rebuilt every twentieth year. Kato gives several interesting native pictures of the shrine and of the ceremonies attending the removal of the Divine Mirror on the occasion of a rebuilding. Whenever the Mikado officiates as high-priest of the nation, he does so in Isé. It is a favourite place for pilgrimages. The pious Shintoist aspires to visit Isé very much as the pious Jew hopes to visit Jerusalem. ' At the present day most Japanese think it a duty to make a

[1] Anesaki, p. 43.

pilgrimage at least once in their life-time to one or more of the most famous Shinto fanes, and believe that their success in life depends upon their doing so. Clubs are formed for the purpose, the subscriptions going to pay the expenses of those fortunate members who are selected to represent their fellows. Pilgrim trains take the place of our excursion trains. Boys and girls frequently run away from home in order to make a pilgrimage to Isé.'[1]

The offerings made by the worshippers consist of the products of the soil and of the sea, such as fish, edible sea-weed, fowls, vegetables, rice and rice-beer (saké), and sometimes the products of the loom. Flowers are not offered, but the green leaves of the tree sakaki. Professor Anesaki sees in this practice a Shinto reaction against the abundant offering of flowers at Buddhist shrines. In pre-historic times, the rite of human sacrifice was practised in Japan but it did not survive the introduction into the country of Confucian ethics and Buddhist precepts of universal benevolence. Thus, during the Tokugawa Régime, we find Yamaga-Soko, the founder of Bushido, saying ' In my humble opinion, offering a human sacrifice to a demon is a custom of the barbarians. It cannot please a true deity, because he refuses to be worshipped with such a false offering. The Emperor Ninkotu did wrong in offering a human sacrifice to the River-god.'[2] In course of time, not only human sacrifice, but also animal sacrifice became repugnant to the Shinto conscience, with the result that all bloody sacrifices are now avoided as involving pollution and food stuffs

[1] Aston, S.A.R.J., p. 63.
[2] Kato, p. 125. See also pp. 104, 124, and 153ff. The fullest treatment of Japanese human sacrifice is by Revon in E.R.E., VI, pp. 855ff. See also E.R.E., VII, p. 146.

are generally offered uncooked. ' In olden times these offerings to the gods included the flesh of the wild animals which the people themselves eat, such as the deer, wild boar, and hare ; when under Buddhist influences, men abandoned a flesh diet, the gods had to give it up too.'[1] The offerings are brought one after another and are raised by the worshipper to his forehead as a mark of reverence. After the ritual has been recited, they are removed by the priest whose perquisite they are. The idea underlying these offerings is that of propitiating the gods, or of expiating offences against them. The simple worshipper expects as a rule some *quid pro quo*, or to be cleansed from his ritual impurity.

The worshipper, of course, offers a prayer, but he does not ' pray for forgiveness of sins, but for the sweet things of this life, for happiness but not for blessedness.'[2] In this connexion something may be said about the place of prayer in Shinto. Few things show the primitive nature of Shinto better than the place and function which it assigns to prayer. The *Kojiki* and the *Nihongi* contain no prayers offered to the deities, and, indeed, scarcely any references to prayer are made by them. In the *Yengi-shiki* we find, however, twenty-five lengthy official litanies (*norito*). These state rituals, written in a fine literary style, belong to a much later period than the *Kojiki* and the *Nihongi*, and were drawn up for the use of the Mikado, or his vicars, on ceremonial occasions. Yet even they contain no petition for moral or spiritual blessings. ' They contain petitions for rain in time of drought, good harvests, preservation from earthquakes

---

[1] Moore, *History of Religions*, I, pp. 103f.
[2] Nitobe, *The Japanese Nation*, p. 124.

and conflagrations, children, health and long life to the sovereign, and enduring peace and prosperity to his rule, the safety of his ambassadors to foreign countries, the suppression of rebellion, the repulse of invasion, success to the Imperial armies, and general prosperity to the Empire.'[1] The *norito* more than once reveal the principle *do ut des*, plainly showing that Shinto prayers are for material blessings. Indeed, their character is magical rather than religious, as we shall see more fully in the next chapter. The point of supreme importance was that the *norito* should be pronounced with perfect accuracy, otherwise its magical virtue would be lost. A great distance ' separates them from the lyrical outbursts that we think of when we speak of prayer properly so called. Even in those *norito* which approach most nearly to formal prayer, the formula is more of the nature of a contract with the gods ; gifts and vague praises are offered to them in exchange for their benefits, and they are promised further rewards if necessary, should their services turn out satisfactory. . . . What the texts never mention is the intimate individual prayer in the inner chamber which the Gospel recommends (Matt. vi, 6). This seems to have had practically no place in the devotions of the primitive Japanese.'[2]

' The common people offer informal prayers to various familiar gods—for example, to Inari, originally the protector of agriculture, then a kind of Japanese Providence, when they are sowing rice or beginning a commercial enterprise, &c. The worshipper who may be seen standing in front of a temple, pulling the white cord that rings a bell to attract the attention of the

[1] Aston, S.W.G., p. 234.   [2] Revon, in E.R.E., X, p. 190.

god, and then praying for a moment with clasped hands, is usually offering a personal petition of the most paltry kind. The more general type of modern prayer asks for " peace to the land, safety to the household and abundant harvest." But modern Shinto prayers, like those of twelve hundred years ago, are always essentially positive, inspired by human wisdom alone ; and, whenever a somewhat elevated moral or mystical idea appears in them, it is the result of Buddhist influence.'[1]

The priests of Shinto do not form a sacerdotal caste, for Shinto has never drawn a clear distinction between the sacred and the secular. The State Shinto rites were in the charge of a Government Bureau, called the *Jingikwan* or ' Department of Religion.' Its officers performed the State cultus and ' its proceedings were as much matters of State as the collection of taxes or the administration of justice.'[2] The Mikado himself is the chief priest of Shinto but for many centuries he has delegated his religious functions, though as late as 1920 he went to Isé to perform the Nihiname. His vicars have always been taken from certain families, or hereditary corporations, who, from ancient times, have claimed the exclusive charge of the State Shinto rites. These are the Nakatomi, the Imbe and the Urabe.

The Nakatomi were the chief officials of the Department of Religion and had control over the Shinto State ceremonies. They recite the *norito* at the festivals and on other solemn occasions. They also exercise some control over the local priesthood. They have been remarkable for the number of poets and statesmen

1 E.R.E., X, p. 191.
2 Aston, in E.R.E., Vol. XI, p. 467.

who have sprung from their ranks, as well as for the number of Imperial consorts they have provided. Tradition, of course, traces their descent from a god. The second hereditary corporation, the Imbe, are credited with a similar lineage. Their duty was to prepare the offerings for sacrifice. *Imi* means religious abstinence, purity ; *Imi-be* means 'religious purity department.' The reference is to the care they must exercise to avoid all impurity when carrying out their duties. The Urabe, the third hereditary corporation, were diviners, who decided by means of their art, such questions as were referred to them by the higher officials of the department of religion. They used the cracks and marks which appear on the shoulder-blade of a deer, or upon a tortoise-shell after it has been held over a fire. The Urabe formed the Japanese counterpart to the Roman college of augurs.

The cultus at the local shrines is in the hands of priests who are called *Kannushi*, that is, *Kami-nushi* or 'deity-master.' These local priests have no cure of souls nor do they receive any special training for their office. It is enough if they recite the prayers and attend to the repairs of the shrine, in which many of them have an hereditary interest. They are at liberty to marry and wear their special dress only when doing duty in the shrine. Hence they are practically indistinguishable from laymen. Their distinctive dress consists of a loose robe with wide sleeves, fastened at the waist with a girdle and a black mitre-like cap bound on to the head with a broad white fillet. This dress is not properly sacerdotal, as it is the old official dress of the Mikado's Court. The *Kannushi* often combine a secular avocation with their priestly functions, which appear to be almost nominal.

In ancient time a virgin princess of royal blood was consecrated to serve as a priestess at the shrine of the Sun-goddess in Isé. There was a similar priestess appointed to the shrine of Kamo near Kyoto, where the Mikado's *Ujigami* (surname-god) was worshipped. Both these offices became extinct some centuries ago. At all the great shrines there is a corps of young girls who are consecrated to the service of the deity. They perform in the sacred pantomimes and render sundry other useful services. On their marriage they resign their office.

Something should now be said about the Ceremonies which form such a conspicuous feature of Shinto. Many, but by no means all, of them are festivals—a term which is sometimes indiscriminately applied to them all. ' Rituals ' is a term which, perhaps, most accurately describes many of them. The *Yengi-shiki* classifies these rituals under three heads :[1] (1) The Greater Ritual, (2) The Middle Rituals, (3) The Lesser Rituals.

The *Oho-nihe* (' Great Tasting ') is placed alone in the first category, because it was regarded as the greatest Shinto ceremony. It gave a solemn religious sanction to the sovereignty of each new Mikado. It was celebrated by each new Emperor in the eleventh month of the year of his accession, or a year later, in order to give time for the elaborate preparations involved. It is, in point of fact, an elaborated version of the annual festival of first-fruits (*Nihi-name*), though it served as a solemn religious ceremony inaugurating the new reign. It corresponds, says Aston, to our coronation ceremony. ' The kernel of this rite was the offering by the Mikado in person to

[1] Kato, pp. 101ff.

the gods, represented by a cushion, of rice and
saké, which were then partaken of by himself and
subsequently by the court.   The rice came from two
provinces selected by divination.   Everything in the
Oho-nihe ceremony was in duplicate, so that, if one
part was vitiated by some accidental impurity, the
other might escape.   Urabe, or diviners, from the
capital superintend the ingathering of the rice, which
was done with great ceremony by a staff of local
officials.   It was then brought to the capital, where
special buildings had been erected for its reception
and for the accommodation of the very numerous
officials concerned.   Here, too, everything was done
in duplicate.   The ceremony included frequent puri-
fications, prayers to the eight gods, which included
amongst others, the harvest gods, the god of growth,
and the food-goddess, and the recital of " ancient
words " and the norito of blessing.'[1]

The Middle Festivals, or rituals of the second class,
are all agricultural festivals, and evidently took shape
after the Japanese people had made the transition
from a life of fishing and hunting to one of agriculture, especially of rice culture.   They are observed
annually.

The Toshigohi (' praying for harvest ') takes place
in the second month of the year when the rice seed is
sown.   The prescribed prayers appeal to practically
all the gods for an abundant harvest.   It ' was celebrated in the chapel of the Imperial Palace by a
Nakatomi as representing the Mikado.'[2]

---

[1] Aston, in E.R.E., Vol. XI, p. 469. See also Moore, *History
of Religions*, Vol. I, p. 104, and for a much longer description,
Aston, S.W.G., pp. 268ff.
[2] Further details and a translation of the *norito* may be found in
Aston, S.W.G., pp. 280ff.

The *Nihi-name* (' new tasting ') is a Harvest Festival or feast of first-fruits. It falls in the eleventh month of the year when the rice of the new harvest was first eaten. The many references to it in the *Nihongi* show it to have originated in a very ancient festival. It is a simpler form of the *Oho-nihe*, ' except that it was performed annually and with much less pomp. Something of the same kind was performed by the local officials and also by the people. Conscientious persons would not eat the new rice until after this celebration.'[1] They felt that before they did so the spirit of the rice must be propitiated.

The Lesser Rituals of the third class include such ceremonies as the following : Praying for abundant rice crops when the rice plants are springing up ; Praying for rain ; Praying to propitiate the Wind-god and to appease the evil deities of epidemic diseases, or to appease the Fire-god ; the Festival of the Road-deities ; the Festival when the *saké*-casks sacred to a certain deity were decorated with wild flowers ; the Spirit-quieting ceremony for ' calming the august spirit,' in other words, for long life for the Emperor.[2]

The *Oho-harahi*, or 'Great Purification' ritual stands somewhat apart from the other rituals and is dealt with in our chapter on ' Ethics.'

At the present time much of this elaborate ritual of Shinto is neglected or stripped of its ancient magnific-ence. For several hundred years previous to the restoration of 1868, ceremonies like the *Oho-harahi* were much neglected by the court.[3] Naturally the

---

[1] E.R.E., Vol. XI, p. 469.
[2] For further details see Aston, S.W.G., pp. 268ff., and E.R.E. article, ' Magic (Japanese).'   [3] cf. E.R.E., X, p. 496.

restoration brought them and many other old forms into prominence again. But, as we shall see later, the revival of Shinto was short-lived and they have again fallen more or less into desuetude. But, as might be expected, the agricultural festivals are still observed by the peasantry.

CHAPTER VI

ETHICS

ANCIENT Shinto is remarkable for the fact that it possesses neither a definite code of morality nor a system of theological dogmas. The complete absence of direct moral teaching in the *Kojiki* and *Nihongi* has already been noticed. This want of an ethical code is hailed by the Shintoist writers as a proof of the superiority of the Japanese people. Thus Motoöri, in the eighteenth century, does not hesitate to say, ' Not only the Mikado, but his ministers and people also, act up to the traditions of the divine age. Hence in ancient times the idea of *Michi*, or way, ethics, was never broached. In ancient times, although there was no prosy system of doctrine in Japan, there were no popular disturbances, and the empire was peacefully ruled. It is because the Japanese were truly moral in their practice that they required no theory of morals. And the fuss made by the Chinese about theoretical morals is owing to their laxity in practice.' Similarly, a present-day Shintoist, Dr. Kato, has no hesitation in admitting that in the ancient Shinto documents the idea of sin is ' more physical than moral ' ; that ' the idea of purity and impurity is merely physical ' ; that ' ancient Shinto has no morality to speak of.'[1] Similarly, Professor K. Ashida says that Shinto has ' never been an ethical factor of much influence.'[2] Nevertheless, in justice to Ancient Shinto, it should

[1] Kato, pp. 112-115.   [2] E.R.E., VII, p. 487.

be said that the rudiments of moral ideas are present in it. Certain offences are enumerated as being hateful to the gods, though they are condemned not so much on moral as on ritual grounds as incurring impurity. The two most famous lists of offences are those found in the *Kojiki* and in the Ritual of the Great Purification. They are in substantial agreement with each other. The *Kojiki* gives the following list of offences : ' flaying alive and flaying backwards, breaking down the divisions of the rice-fields, filling up ditches, marriages between superiors and inferiors, marriages with horses, marriages with cattle, marriages with fowls, and marriages with dogs.' The Ritual of the Great Purification distinguishes between ' Heavenly Offences ' and ' Earthly Offences.' The Heavenly Offences, according to the Ritual are : ' the breaking down of divisions between rice-fields, filling up irrigation channels, removing water-pipes, sowing seed over again, planting skewers (or wands), flaying alive, flaying backwards, evacuating excrementa.' The Earthly Offences are : ' the cutting of living bodies, the cutting of dead bodies, leprosy, *kokumi* (probably a skin disease), incest of a man with his mother or daughter, with his mother-in-law or step-daughter, bestiality, calamities from creeping things (snakes, centipedes, &c.), calamities through the gods on high, through the birds on high, killing animals, bewitchments.' These two lists obviously take us back to a fairly primitive stage in the evolution of ethical ideas. Theft, adultery, and fornication are not mentioned ; nor are many other actions which would be regarded as sins, or offences, by the enlightened conscience.

The division of offences into two classes (Heavenly and Earthly) is noteworthy and is not to be so simply

5

explained as Aston suggests. According to him, it is due to the author of the Ritual adopting the rhetorical device of two balanced sentences in order to break up a long list of offences.[1] Revon is on sounder lines in suggesting[2] that the Heavenly Offences were so called because they are the very ones which, according to mythology, were committed in heaven by the wicked god, Susa-no-wo, against the Sun-goddess.

It is significant that in the forefront of the list of Heavenly Offences stand crimes which would be held most reprehensible by a people engaged in the cultivation of rice. The meaning of ' sowing seed over again ' will be clear to all familiar with the Parable of the Wheat and Tares (Matt. xiii, 24-30). Planting skewers or wands in the rice-fields is probably a magical practice, as is also flaying an animal alive or backwards. Probably some evil use was made of the skins so obtained. The Earthly Offences are mostly physical pollutions and sexual offences such as incest and bestiality. One or two require comment here in order to make their meaning clear. ' Cutting living bodies,' which includes murder and wounding, is regarded as defiling because every effusion of blood is polluting even to the victim. Even justifiable homicide causes uncleanness. Wounds, whether inflicted or received, were objectionable, not on humanitarian grounds, but because they defiled. ' Cutting of dead bodies ' is polluting because contact with a corpse brings defilement. ' Calamities from the gods on high ' doubtless refers to lightning. ' Calamities from birds on high ' refers to the possibility of food being polluted by the droppings of birds falling through the hole in the roof by which the smoke escapes. ' Killing animals '

[1] Aston, S.W.G., p. 300.   [2] E.R.E., XI, p. 566.

Revon takes to mean, 'not animals in general, as in
Buddhism, but only the domestic animals of one's
neighbours, perhaps by means of evil spells.'[1]

We are now in a position to summarize the ideas of
sin in Ancient Shinto. It is clear that the Heavenly
and Earthly Offences of the Ritual of the Great
Purification really cover, not two, but three distinct
classes of offences, namely, ill deeds, uncleanness and
calamities. Of these three categories only the first
corresponds in any way to the Christian idea of sin.
But Ancient Shinto looked upon uncleanness and
calamities as sins or offences because it drew no
distinction between moral faults and ritual impurity,
even when the latter was a calamity quite inadvertently incurred. The Ritual is quite explicit that the
offences it catalogues are offences whether committed
'inadvertently or deliberately.' No account is taken
of the offender's intention. There is here no ethic of
conscience. 'The notion of purely moral sin, as we
conceive it, did not gain supremacy in Japan until
Buddhism was introduced, which . . . brought a new
morality founded no longer on ancient magic, but on
the discriminations of conscience.'[2]

Shinto was dominated by a great fear of uncleanness in the external and ceremonial sense of the term.
Uncleanness could be contracted in many ways, for
example, by contact with blood, diseases and corpses,
and by incest and bestiality. Menstrual blood was
specially defiling.[3] The consummation of a marriage
caused defilement and therefore in ancient times a
special hut was provided for the purpose, so that
the house might not be defiled. Childbirth caused

[1] E.R.E., XI, p. 567. [2] Revon, in E.R.E., XI, p. 567.
[3] Kato, p. 114.

uncleanness and therefore special parturition huts were
provided for women about to be delivered of a child.
Contact with a corpse caused uncleanness. When
Izanagi returned from his visit to Hades, he lost no
time before he purified himself with water by plunging
into a stream. A death in a house rendered it unclean.
It was abandoned by the survivors. This explains
why the capital was changed with every new emperor
down to the year A.D. 710.[1] To-day this idea has been
modified and the emperors retain a permanent home.
Impurity is also incurred by the death of a relative,
by eating food in a house of mourning, by attending a
funeral, pronouncing or executing a death-sentence.
' According to the strict Shinto of a later period, a man
must abstain from worship at a shrine for thirty days
if he has wounded somebody, or, if he has accidentally
hurt himself, so that more than three drops of blood
have flowed, for that day. If he has vomited or
passed blood, he must not worship for two days, if he
has an abscess, until it is cured, for seven days after
moxa is applied, and for three days in the case of the
operator. At the present day the common word for
wound is *kega*, that is to say, defilement.'[2] The
eating of flesh was not regarded as causing uncleanness
but Buddhist influences brought a change. According
to the *Yengi-shiki*, those who eat the flesh of beasts
are unclean for three days.

This ritual pollution, of course, debarred a man or
woman from taking part in Shinto worship. According
to the *Yengi-shiki*, ' pollution from human death shall
debar for thirty days from the date of the funeral ;
pollution from human birth for seven days ; pollution
from animal death for five days ; and from animal

[1] cf. Anesaki, p. 86. [2] Aston, S.W.G., p. 253.

birth, not including chickens, for three days. Those who ate the flesh of beasts were impure for three days. Participation in the reburial of the dead rendered one impure for four months or longer. Those who had attended a funeral, visited the sick, or been present at a memorial service were forbidden to enter the royal gate on the same day.'[1]

When the state of purity had been lost it could only be regained by ritual performances. Hence the prominence given to rites of purification. Of these, the Great Purification (*Oho-harahi*) is much the most important. It was celebrated twice a year, at the end of June and the end of December. It was intended to cleanse the community from all pollution incurred since its last celebration. By virtue of the rite all evils and impurities were purged away. It was usually performed at the southern gate of the royal palace in Kyoto and simultaneously at various Shinto shrines.

The ritual of the Great Purification was fairly simple. A Nakatomi, on behalf of the Mikado, recited the tenth *norito*[2] of the *Yengi-shiki*. The recital of this *norito*, which is called ' the powerful ritual words of the celestial ritual,' was supposed to have an intrinsic, magical virtue. ' When the high-priest recites it thus, according to the text of the ritual itself, the gods of heaven and earth will approach to listen, and all offences will disappear, being swept off, carried away to the ocean by the goddess of the torrents, swallowed by the goddess of the sea-currents, driven to the nether regions by the god whose breath chases before it all impurities, and there they will be seized at last by a subterranean deity who will banish them for ever.'[3]

---

[1] E.R.E., X, p. 496.   [2] Trans. in Aston, S.W.G., pp. 296ff.
[3] E.R.E., VIII, p. 298.

In order to make matters more certain, the reading of
the magical formula was accompanied by the offering
of certain ransom-objects, which the diviners (*urabe*)
afterwards threw into the river, the idea being that the
offences of the people would disappear along with the
objects to which they had been transferred. The
norito concluded with the following formula of
absolution :

> ' As the many-piled clouds of Heaven are scattered by
> the breath of the Wind-Gods : as the morning breezes and
> the evening breezes dissipate the dense morning vapours
> and the dense evening vapours : as a huge ship, moored
> in a great harbour, casting off its stern-moorings, casting
> off its bow-moorings, drives forth into the great sea-plain :
> as yonder thick brushwood is smitten and cleared away
> by the sharp sickle forged in the fire—so shall all offences
> be utterly annulled.'

In addition to the Great Purification Ceremony,
there were other means, constantly available, by which
the follower of Shinto could rid himself of his impurity.
The one most frequently used was lustration in
water. To-day there is in the court before a Shinto
shrine a laver, generally of stone, in which the worshippers wash their hands before prayer. Salt was
also used as a medium for dispelling impurity. This
was, no doubt, because its antiseptic qualities were
known. Writing in 1905, Aston says that ' at the
entrances to theatres at the present day a saucer of
salt is placed on a table in order to keep out evil
influences.'[1] Spitting was a symbolic, and therefore
effective, means of expelling impurity. It was also
thought that defilement could be transferred by
breathing on some object which was afterwards cast
into the sea. Small dolls in paper or metal were cast

1 Aston, S.W.G., p. 260.

into a river or the sea and were thought to carry away the pollution of the people in a time of pestilence.[1] ' So persistent are the primitive notions that in relatively modern times they have given rise to a new custom quite in the ancient spirit. A few days before the semi-annual *Oho-harahi*, a man or woman who wishes to be purified procures from the temple a small piece of white paper cut rudely in the shape of a skirt. On this he writes his name, sex, the year and month of his birth, rubs the paper over his whole body, and breathes into it, thus transferring to it his sins or ailments, and brings it back to the temple, where the collection is deposited on a black table during the purification ceremony, and at the end is sent off in a boat and thrown into the water.'[2]

Enough has been said to show that Ancient Shinto moved on that lower cultural and ethical level on which no clear distinction was drawn between defilement, disease and guilt, or between intentional sins and inadvertent ritual offences. Defilement, sin and guilt were, moreover, all believed to be transmissible and removable by physical or magical means. Its notion of purity was ceremonial and pre-ethical. Purity was a negative state rather than a positive ideal. It was the state which resulted from the avoidance of those intentional and inadvertent acts which cause defilement. Like most primitive peoples, the ancient Japanese connected ceremonial defilement with the crises of human life, such as birth, marriage and death. Their notion of ceremonial purity was closely bound up with the concept of *tabu*. A man in a state of impurity was regarded as dangerous not only to himself but also to all other members of the

[1] Kato, p. 115. [2] Moore, *History of Religions*, Vol. I, pp. 106f.

community, whom he might infect with his own uncleanness. Hence restrictions were placed upon him.
He was isolated and his actions were regulated until he
had purified himself by the appropriate ceremony,
which was regarded as having a magical efficacy. As
Shinto took no account of the offender's intentions,
so it found no place for inward repentance as a means
of expiation or of restoring a right relation to the gods.
It employed the same mediums of purification as those
used by most primitive peoples, such as water, trans-
ference of impurity, substitution of an expiatory
victim. Of water, the commonest of these mediums,
it made great use. But whereas in the higher religions,
washing in water has only a symbolic or sacramental
significance, in Shinto, as in the lower religions, it was
thought actually to remove the impurity. Indeed,
the whole process of purification is on the level of the
magical ; the rites are thought of as working *ex opere
operato*. We should, however, do less than justice to
Shinto, if we did not concede that the firm emphasis
which it laid upon ceremonial purity and upon
lustrations in water has contributed something valuable
to the life of the Japanese people, who are known for
their personal cleanliness. Nor need we doubt that
the elementary ethical notions, with which we have
been concerned in this chapter, would have developed
into something higher but for the fact that Buddhist
and Confucian influences intervened to arrest their
development.

Mention should be made of the contribution made
by the cult of the Mikado to the development of
ethical ideas in Japan. This cult of necessity stressed
the virtue of submission ; but it was a submission
that demanded action and valour. Hence the militant

aspect of Japanese morality, which introduces us to that peculiar creation of Japan, the Bushido ethical code.

Bushido (The Way of the Warrior) was the result of the impact of Confucian ethics upon Japan, where conditions were very different from those in China. In China the primary relation is that between father and son ; in Japan it is between ruler and subject. In China the first virtue was filial piety ; in Japan it was loyalty to the emperor. In China peace was the first desideratum and the scholar stood highest in the social scale ; in Japan peace was never regarded as a primary consideration and the first man in the land has been the Samurai, who unites in his person the soldier and the scholar, two rôles always kept apart in China. Thus when Confucian ethical ideals came into Japan they underwent a modification and one result was the evolution of the Bushido code of morals. Buddhist influences were also an integral factor, while Shinto inculcated the central notion of loyalty. Bushido was elaborated by the Samurai or knights in the twelfth century, when the decay of imperial power led to feudal wars. Its ideals and teaching swayed the ruling classes from that time to the end of the feudal régime in 1868. Bushido represents the ideals of chivalry which came to prevail among the nobles. It differs from the European Chivalry of the later middle ages in laying great stress upon quietness and sternness of manner in contrast to the gallantry of its nearest European counterpart.

The key-note of Bushido is loyalty to one's emperor and feudal lord. Life itself is to be held of little value compared with steadfastness in maintaining one's allegiance. Coupled with loyalty were hardness and stoic indifference to death. Hence the exaltation of suicide (*harakiri*) and the saying that the sword is the soul of the Samurai, who must commit suicide when death alone can save his honour. Simplicity and frugality form part of the Bushido ideal, as also do serenity, sincerity, courage, self-sacrifice, self-control, proper decorum, magnanimity and bold idealism. ' In short, religious beliefs and worldly wisdom, spiritual teaching and military discipline, moral ideals and practical counsels, these were fused into one principle of the warrior's honour.'[1]

Naturally Shinto writers lavish praise upon the moral virtues which Bushido has fostered. There is, however, another side to the picture, to which Professor Anesaki points in the following words: ' In a conspicuous contrast to the height of her influence in the reign of Buddhist sentimentalism, a characteristic feature of Bushido was the debasement of woman and the consequent contempt for love and affection in general. The rise of the military men, together with Confucian ethics, led to the degradation of the position and dignity of woman in social life . . . Any sign of undue respect towards her on the part of a man was denounced as disgraceful to him, especially to a Samurai.'[2]

Professor Knox calls attention to two other defects in Bushido. (*a*) In spite of the virtues it inculcated Bushido left the warrior free to practise any deceit or fraud for the sake of overcoming his enemy. ' The righteousness was that of the soldier, which is tolerant of the errors of private life, but requires instant, complete and unquestionable obedience.' Hence the

[1] Anesaki, p. 222.   [2] Anesaki, pp. 286f.

stories told of 'righteous samurai,' who debauched themselves, divorced wife, drove away children, and wasted their substance in low pleasures, in order that they might throw their enemy off his guard and accomplish their deed of vengeance. (b) 'With the exaltation of self-sacrifice and the thorough-going subordination of the individual to the organization, the value of the individual is depreciated and a vigorous personality is not developed. For there is in the individual no most holy place which may not be violated, but daughter and son are to go to all lengths for the sake of parent or lord. A popular preacher can take as illustration of the very con-summation of holiness a daughter who sells herself to a house of ill-fame so as to procure medicine for her father who is ill, without a word of reproach for the parent who accepts the gift.'[1]

Something may here be said in more detail about *harakiri*, since it is a purely Japanese practice of considerable antiquity. Literally *harakiri* means ' belly-cut ' and consists in making a horizontal or cruciform cut in the abdomen. It was often nothing more than one form of suicide or an honourable form of execution. As such it must be distinguished from the *harakiri* which the Samurai in certain circum-stances deemed to be their duty. As a matter of fact, *harakiri* is a vulgar expression which a Samurai would have been ashamed to use. He called his peculiar method of suicide *seppuku*.[2] According to Dr. T. Harada, *seppuku* dates from the twelfth century and was developed into a system with much etiquette and

---

[1] Knox, pp. 152f. The curious may find more information on Bushido in E.R.E., IV, p. 895, V, p. 499, VII, p. 486 ; Anesaki, pp. 262ff ; Knox, pp. 149ff.   [2] Anesaki, p. 264n.

formality during the Tokugawa period. ' It was not mere suicide. It was an institution, legal and ceremonial, invented in the middle ages, by which warriors could expiate their crimes, apologize for error, escape from disgrace, redeem their friends or prove their sincerity.'[1]

The best known example of *harakiri* in modern times is the suicide of Count Nogi, who, in September, 1912, at the time of the funeral of the Emperor, put himself to death that he might follow his sovereign into the next world. The Countess Nogi also killed herself that she might follow her husband. ' On this occasion Japanese opinion was by no means unanimous with regard to the social utility of this act, which, though putting a harmonious completion to the life of a warrior of the old school, deeply imbued with the ancient traditions of loyalty, deprived the Japanese nation of a man of experience on whose services it could have depended should new dangers arise from outside. The police of Tokyo, however, had to take measures to prevent this suicide being imitated by contagion.'[2] The special name given to suicide upon the death of one's lord, master or husband with a view to following them into the next world, is *junshi*, i.e. ' following in death.'

To save Shinto from the reproach of being entirely lacking in ethical teaching, modern apologists for Shinto often point to passages in which the virtue of sincerity is inculcated. Thus Dr. Kato says that in his opinion ' Aston may be right in saying that ancient Shinto has no moral teachings to speak of,' but he

---

[1] E.R.E., XII, p. 36. In this article Dr. Harada quotes elaborate statistics showing that Japan is a country in which an unusual number commit suicide.　　　[2] E.R.E., VI, p. 857.

thinks ' the germs of morality ' can be found in some of the traditions of the *Kojiki* and the *Nihongi*.[1] Next, Dr. Kato invites us to ' see how this seed of morality grew into the great tree of the Shinto ethical system, under which birds of the air may find rest for themselves ' and proceeds to cite such passages as the following :

> ' What pleases the Deity is virtue and sincerity, and not any number of material offerings.'
> ' Gods or Spirits are impartial and just in mind, pleased only with a man's religious piety. Approach and pray to them with a sincere heart, and be sure that you will thus gain their favour.'
> ' The surest passport for entrance into communion with the Divine is sincerity. If you pray to the Deity with sincerity, you will assuredly realize the divine presence.'[2]

What Dr. Kato fails to do is to call his readers' attention to the fact that the passages he cites are all comparatively late and belong to the period when Buddhist and Confucian ethics had profoundly modified Shinto and supplied motives and ideals for individual, private conduct and thus had remedied an inherent defect of Ancient Shinto.

Dr. R. D. M. Shaw, who has had the advantage of residence in Japan, calls attention to two directions in which present-day Shinto is endeavouring to deepen its ethical teaching. (1) In Ancient Shinto what the worshipper feared was that he might approach the divine in a ritually unworthy manner. The modern Shintoist, however, is taught that, in addition to

---

[1] p. 152. The few instances he cites are not very convincing. He would have done better to call attention to the two passages from the *Nihongi* cited by Hume in his *The World's Living Religions*, p. 162.
[2] Kato, pp. 161, 163. Other passages of a like nature may be found in Aston, S.W.G., p. 369.

respecting ritual requirements, he must be morally
worthy when he approaches the divine spirits. ' This
is illustrated by the teaching or custom which is
growing up in connexion with the central symbol of
the Shinto shrine (the round metal mirror) . . . The
Shinto worshipper is told to do reverence to this
symbol, not merely by doing obeisance before it, but
by looking into it, seeing there the reflection of his
own self, and from his own reflection inferring the
presence of his ancestors in whose likeness he has been
made. Thus he is to remind himself not to bring
disgrace upon his ancestors by any dishonourable
conduct. He is to be morally worthy to approach
the divine spirits . . . In Shinto, therefore, the fear
which was originally limited to ritual matters has been
spiritualized and ethicized.' (2) The changing conception of the nature of man's approach to the divine
is modifying the conception of his means of approach
also. ' The new tendency shows itself in the enforce-
ment of the ideas of filial piety and loyalty—and
especially of the latter virtue. These two duties have
always been implicit in the very idea of ancestor
worship, but in modern Shinto they have become a
sine quâ non of admission to fellowship with the spirits.
Shinto to-day cannot consider any one being considered
worthy of admission to the worship of the ancestral
spirits who is not prepared to offer his very life in their
service. This is the explanation of the self-sacrificing
heroism of the Japanese soldier, and of the self-
immolation of such a great man as General Nogi and
his wife . . . These are the duties which are continually
enforced by the reading of Imperial rescripts, and they
form the basis of all the moral instruction which is
given in the schools. Shinto is relegating the idea of

ritual purity into the background, and bringing forward moral duties, especially those of filial piety and loyalty, as the proper means of attaining a character worthy of admission to the service of the great ancestral spirits of the nation.'[1]

1 *Enlightenment and Salvation*, pp. 32-34.

CHAPTER VII

MAGIC, DIVINATION, &c.

In his article on Magic (Japanese) in the *Encyclopædia of Religion and Ethics*, Revon has convincingly proved his thesis that magic exists ' in the very heart of the national religion, in the most authentic documents of pure Shinto.' He has carefully examined the *norito* collected in the *Yengi-shiki* and has shown that it is virtually a mistake to call these *norito* prayers. They are much rather ' magical formulæ, solemn incantations . . . enveloped in powerful rites by which the magician priests of primitive Japan conquered their gods.' Revon calls rather special attention to the eighth *norito*. Its title ' Luck-bringer of the Great Palace ' indicates its magical nature. Indeed, this ritual is defined in its own text as ' the celestial magical protective words.' ' It is a formula,' says Revon, ' the recitation of which wards off all calamity from the palace, as an amulet would do ; this is shown by the importance ascribed to the perfect regularity of the words pronounced ; for, in another passage, certain " corrector "-gods are begged to rectify all omissions that they may have seen or heard in the rites or the words of the ceremony.' The rite includes the magical use of rice and jewels to combat evil influences. A retinue of priests (both *nakatomi* and *imibe*) and vestals goes through all the rooms of the palace, from the great audience room even to the Emperor's privy. The vestals sprinkle the rooms visited with rice and *saké*, while the *imibe* hang precious stones on the four corners of the rooms. The ritual scattering of rice is a frequent magical practice in Shinto. It was scattered inside the parturition hut just before a woman's confinement. It may have been simply a bait thrown to the demons, or it may have been a piece of apotropaic magic. The shape of the grain has caused it (like the bean) to be regarded in Japan as a synonym for the *vulva*. The idea underlying the throwing of rice may, therefore, be that, as a symbol of generative power, its vital force overcomes illness and death. It was thought that the jewels paraded in the imperial apartments would cause the dark threats of the invisible to retire before their brightness.

To continue Revon's demonstration of the predominant part played by magic in the Shinto ceremonies, we may mention that in the eleventh ritual the Emperor was ' presented with a silver-gilt human effigy, which would play the part of scapegoat by removing calamities from him, and a gilded sword on which he breathed before it was taken from him, with the same intention of driving away, after this magical transfer, both the sins committed and their material support.' The fifteenth *norito*, for ' calming the august spirit,' is simply a magical means ' of keeping the imperial soul in the Emperor's body, of recalling it if it seemed to wish to escape—in a word, of renewing magically the vital force of the sovereign for the coming year and thus prolonging his life.' In another similar rite a *nakatomi* knotted threads, which were obviously meant to retain the imperial soul. After they had been knotted he shut them up in a closed vessel. Jewels appear again in the twenty-seventh

6

norito, which is really a rite for bringing happiness to the Emperor. The magical rôle of the jewels is clearly referred to in the following words : ' These white jewels are the great august white hairs (to which your Majesty will reach) ; the red jewels are the august, healthful, ruddy countenance.' The different jewels have a power corresponding to their colour. Like produces like, according to the fundamental principle of imitative magic.

Divination[1] is an ancient magical practice in Japan as the *Kojiki* and *Nihongi* abundantly show. ' For the Japanese, the idea of divination does not necessarily involve a prediction, but only the discovery of something hidden—present, past or future. It may be employed not only to find out whether such and such an event will occur in the future, whether it will be lucky or the opposite, &c., but also to reveal the present will of the gods on such and such a point, and even to discover why a certain event—generally an untoward one—has occurred in the past.' At certain important points of Shinto worship divination was regularly employed. By divination the priestess of the Sun was chosen at Isé ; the ceremonial purity of those taking part in religious rites was ascertained ; and the provinces selected from which the sacred rice should be taken for use in the Festival of the Great Tasting. The magical character of Shinto divination is seen by the fact that in the ancient records the gods themselves are represented as having found it necessary to resort to it—a fact which gave some trouble to Pure Shintoists like Hirata.[2]

[1] The subject is elaborately treated by Revon in E.R.E., IV. pp. 80Iff. What is said here is taken from his article.
[2] See below, pp. 97ff.

Revon calls attention to the distinction between the
official procedure (The Greater Divination) and other
secondary or minor forms of divination. The ' Greater
Divination ' consisted of *omoplatoscopy*—a fairly wide-
spread practice among primitive peoples. The
shoulder-blade of a deer was held over a bright fire
and the cracks produced by the heat were carefully
noted. At an early date the upper shell of a tortoise
was substituted for the deer's shoulder-blade. The
influence of Chinese practices may here be suspected
but the change would be facilitated by the place
occupied by the tortoise in Shinto mythology.

Secondary, or non-official, divination had many
forms, of which the following may be noted. ' Cross-
roads divination ' was practised, according to the
Manyo-shiu, chiefly by women and lovers. The person
employing it went to the cross-roads at dusk, planted
a stick in the ground, and then took the remarks of
the passers-by as an answer to what he wanted to
know. In a variation of this kind of divination the
women went to the nearest cross-roads, drew a line of
demarcation on the road and sprinkled it with rice,
which, as we have just seen, was a powerful agent
against evil spirits. Then each woman made a
box-wood comb to sound three times by passing a
finger along its teeth. This was a means of inviting
the god to speak. After this, they would listen for the
words of the first person who came within the enchanted
circle and draw an answer therefrom. In ' Bridge-
divination ' the same processes were employed on
a bridge instead of at the cross-roads. ' Stone-
divination ' consisted in foretelling the future from the
apparent weight of a stone when lifted up. ' Divination by gruel ' was a local practice, confined apparently

to the temple of Kasuga. Its purpose was to find out
what kinds of vegetables and cereals it would be best
to sow for the year. A pot was placed before the
gods and in it were boiled some special red beans,
whose colour suggested health and victory over the
demons of disease. Fifty-four tubes of reed or
bamboo, each bearing the name of one of the vegetables
it was proposed to cultivate, were then plunged into
the gruel. The priests then withdrew the tubes with
chopsticks and derived their prognostics from the
manner in which the gruel went into the tubes. The
peasants then sowed their seed according to these
indications. ' Caldron-divination ' foretells the future
from the sounds made by a boiling caldron. Divination by drawing lots is quite common to this day.[1]

The ordeal, which is really a specialized form of
divination, was in use in ancient Japan. There are
references in the *Kojiki* and *Nihongi* to the fire-ordeal
and the ordeal by boiling-water. The serpent-ordeal
goes back to ancient times. According to the *Kojiki*,
Susa-no-wo subjected his future son-in-law to this test
by making him sleep in the hut of serpents and then
in the hut of centipedes. He escaped by the help of
the magic scarfs of Princess Suseri.

Omens and dreams may here be mentioned. ' These
come under divination, even though in them we are
not dealing, in principle, with processes involving the
active initiative of man, but only with spontaneous
facts, outside of man, for which he seeks an interpretation after they have occurred.'[2] White and red
animals were regarded by the *Nihongi* as of good omen,

---

[1] In E.R.E., IV, p. 804, may be found some curious and
interesting information by Revon about divination in modern
Japan.   [2] Revon, in E.R.E., IV, p. 805.

because of their rarity and because they harmonized with the favourite colours of a solar religion like Shinto. The same text speaks of the visit of an owl or wren to a parturition hut as a good omen. The ill omens mentioned in the *Kojiki* and *Nihongi* are too numerous to catalogue. They include such things as earth-quakes, floods, comets, a prolonged eclipse of the sun, the mysterious movements of a swarm of flies.

Dreams are often recorded in the *Kojiki* and *Nihongi* as omens and as giving knowledge of the future, when skilfully interpreted.

The *Kojiki* and *Nihongi* make frequent reference to gods and men being ' possessed ' or inspired by the supernatural. The Japanese word, *kangakari* (literally ' god-attachment ') ' expresses the idea of the passive attitude of a man under a superior influence which takes possession of him.'[1] Naturally it was assumed that oracles could be obtained from persons thus ' possessed.' The person in this state served as a medium and those in quest of information addressed to him their questions. Thus we have in this practice a secondary method of divination, which was regarded with some mistrust by the court and the upper Shinto clergy, who were faithful to the official method of the ' Greater Divination.' As a result, though possession played an important part in the most ancient Shinto, it tended, at a later date, to become a popular pro-ceeding, more and more neglected by the official religion.

Amulets [2] are common in Japan. The people hang them up on the door-ways of their houses or carry

[1] Revon, in E.R.E., X, p. 131 (article ' Possession-Japanese '), from which what is said here is taken.

[2] Much detail in E.R.E., III, pp. 449-451, but the article does not sufficiently distinguish between Shinto and Buddhism.

them on their persons. They may be bought at most of the shrines. They are used to ward off sickness, demons, bewitchment and ill-luck; to prevent accidents; to protect houses, crops and domestic animals; and to ward off the dangers of pregnancy and childbirth.

Many of the foregoing magical practices of Shinto continue to this day. Indeed, they have been combined with and elaborated by Buddhist occultism. Japan is a land of much superstition. ' It is as omnipresent, as persistent, as hard to kill as the scrub bamboo which both efficiently and sufficiently takes the place of thorns and thistles as the curse of Japanese ground.'[1] The will of General Count Nogi, whose dramatic suicide was noticed above, offered his body to the Faculty of Medicine for scientific purposes. But he made one reservation. His teeth, hair and nails were to be buried. Even in him we see the survival of conceptions belonging to the ages of primitive magic.[2]

[1] Griffis, p. 12.
[2] See E.R.E., VI, p. 857. In his *Enlightenment and Salvation*, p. 33, R. D. M. Shaw calls attention to the fact that there is no ' black magic ' in Shinto.

CHAPTER VIII

THE DECAY OF SHINTO

SHINTO, which had enjoyed an unchallenged supremacy in Japan from time immemorial, found itself faced for the first time with a rival faith, when Buddhism was introduced into Japan in the year A.D. 552. In that year a deputation from a Korean prince arrived at the Japanese Court bringing with it Buddhist priests, statues of the Buddha and his saints, copies of some of the Buddhist Scriptures, banners and other articles used in Buddhist worship. These presents were accompanied with the following messages :

'This religion is the most excellent of all teachings, though difficult to master and hard to comprehend ; even the sages of China would have found it not easy to grasp. It brings endless and immeasurable blessings and fruits (to its believers), even the attainment of the supreme enlightenment. Just as the *Chinta-mani* jewel is said to fulfil every need according to desire, so the treasure of this glorious religion will never cease to give full response to those who seek for it. Moreover, the religion has come over to Korea far from India, and the peoples (in the countries between these two) are now ardent followers of its teaching, and none are outside its pale.'[1]

The *Nihongi* gives a graphic picture of the division of opinion among the Mikado's ministers when he asked them whether the new worship should be received or not. One minister, the head of the Soga family, who were administrators and diplomats and who felt the need of a progressive policy, answered in

[1] Anesaki, p. 53.

the affirmative. Another minister, who was the head
of the Mononobe family, who were military clansmen
and contemptuous of foreign importations, declared
' If we were to worship foreign deities, it may be feared
that we should incur the wrath of our national gods.'
The priestly family, the Nakatomi, were naturally
at this time anti-Buddhist, though some of their
descendants at a later time became devoted Buddhists.
In the end, the Mikado ordered the image of Buddha
to be given to the minister Soga, who was to make the
experiment of worshipping it. This he did in his
own home but when a pestilence broke out, the anti-
Buddhist ministers obtained permission to have the
image thrown into a canal.

The conservatives, however, were fighting a losing
battle. What made the appeal of Buddhism so strong
was the fact that it came into Japan as part and parcel
of the higher civilization of China, which was then
penetrating Japan and being rapidly assimilated by
the Japanese. ' The first presentation of Buddhist
objects was followed by a continual influx of missionaries, artisans and other immigrants, reinforcing the
influence of the new religion. The introduction,
furthermore, of the medical science, of Chinese arts
and sciences, especially of writing and astronomy, was
always identified with Buddhist missions, and even the
conservatives gradually gave in to the irresistible
force of these importations.'[1] It is abundantly clear
that we must look upon the spread of Buddhism in
Japan as an integral part of the acceptance by the
Japanese people of the higher culture of China. The
adoption of a new and higher civilization meant also
the adoption of a new and higher type of religion,

[1] Aneskai, p. 55.

which, in accordance with the genius of the Japanese people, was constantly adjusted by them to meet their temperament and needs.

By A.D. 589 the progressive Soga family had overcome their rivals and the way was open for Buddhism to make a rapid advance. In 593 they placed on the throne an empress who was a devoted Buddhist. The real ruler of the country was Shotoku, her nephew, whom the empress appointed Prince-Regent. With the support of the progressives he ruled for thirty years and his reign marks the rapid advance in Japan of Buddhist influences and Chinese civilization. Shotoku was an ardent Buddhist, learned in the Buddhist Scriptures but also in the writings of Confucius and Mencius. He sent to China a number of monks and students to study, not only Buddhist philosophy but also the political philosophy of Confucius and Chinese methods of government. On their return these students were leaders in the re-organization of the Japanese system of government on the Chinese model. The ancient clan system was replaced by a strongly centralized government, with eight ministerial departments, and a hierarchy of officials, whose functions were carefully defined. Successive codes were put out, all of which make it clear that Chinese models were being followed. The definitive code of 702 was even promulgated in the Chinese language. Some of these codes are, of course, much later than Shotoku but he is the ruler to whom the Japanese rightly look back as the pioneer of the movement for the adoption of Buddhism and a higher type of civilization and administration.

In 604, in connexion with his task of reforming the internal administration of Japan, Shotoku issued a proclamation setting forth the ideas and ideals which, in his opinion, should control the administration of the country. His proclamation is known as ' Constitution in Seventeen Articles.' Though issued to all the populace it was designed for the instruction of the state-officials, whom Shotoku wished to see imbued with those lofty ideals of official obligations and responsibility which he had found in the Chinese classics. The Second Article is noteworthy for its strong commendation of Buddhism. His people are bidden to venerate sincerely ' The Three Treasures,' namely, the Buddha, the Dhamma and the Sangha, which are said by Shotoku to be ' the final resort of all beings and the supreme object of faith for all peoples.'

In many respects the reign of the Emperor Shomu (A.D. 724-748) marks the highest peak of Buddhist influence. He began to erect in Nara a great Buddhist temple, in which the Buddha is represented by a colossal bronze figure,[1] which is said to be still the largest bronze figure in the world. This was successfully cast in 749. It is more than fifty feet in height and represents the Buddha as seated on a lotus. ' The enormous halo is studded with minor statues of Buddhas and saints, while on the petals of the pedestal are engraved scenes of the twenty-five realms of existence with figures of celestial and terrestrial beings—all united in adoration of the central figure and glorifying the majesty of the Supreme Enlightened.'[2] ' The dedication of the completed structure (in 752) was the most brilliant event in the history of Japanese

---

[1] Such a colossal image is known in Japan as Daibutsu (Great Buddha). The one at Nara is still standing after many repairs. For its history see E.R.E., IV, pp. 388ff.
[2] Anesaki, p. 89.

Buddhism. The whole court attended the ceremony
and thousands of priests are said to have participated
in it. The gilded statue stood in the centre, the ceil-
ings and pillars were lavishly decorated, golden
banners and variegated curtains waved in the air,
candles illuminated the altars and niches. All sorts
of music and dances were performed, introduced from
India, Annam, China and Korea. The richness and
splendour of the ceremony can be imagined from the
relics of objects used on the occasion, preserved even
to this day . . . scores of dance masks, numerous
musical instruments elaborately decorated with mother-
of-pearl, rich brocades and fine needlework of varied
designs, and screens originally decorated with iridescent
feathers, which were set up by the road-side leading
from the palace to the temple.'[1]

In connexion with the dedication of the above
mentioned temple, we find the beginnings of what
came to be known as Ryobu, or 'Double Aspect'
Shinto. Ryobu Shinto is an amalgam of Buddhism
and Shinto. A Buddhist priest named Gyogi was
sent to the temple of the Sun-goddess in Isé to present
to her a Buddhist relic and to inquire of her how she
viewed the Emperor's project of a colossal image of
the Buddha. Gyogi brought back an oracle which
was interpreted to mean that the Sun-goddess was
identical with, or a manifestation of, the Buddha
Vairochana (who, in some Buddhist sects, occupies
an exalted station among the transcendental Buddhas
similar to that occupied by Amaterasu among the
Shinto deities) and gave her sanction to the Emperor's
project. This is the first instance of the application
by Buddhist missionaries of the principle they had

[1] Anesaki, p. 90. See also E.R.E., IV, pp. 388ff.

already adopted in China of identifying the native gods of the country with one of their many Buddhas or saints. They declared that the gods of Shinto were incarnations of the various Buddhas. This is the basic principle of Ryobu Shinto, which is simply Buddhistic Shinto.

The chief exponent of Ryobu Shinto was Kobo Daishi (A.D. 774-835), the founder of the Shingon School of Buddhism. His system is thoroughly syncretistic but is much more Buddhist than Shinto. He taught that the Buddhist deities[1] were the originals of which the Shinto deities were their earthly counterparts or manifestations. ' The Buddhist pantheon in general was thought to represent the Indestructibles, while the deities of the Shinto pantheon were interpreted as their partial manifestations . . . In carrying out this combination or parallelism, every *Kami* was regarded as a manifestation of a certain Buddhist deity, and the majority of the Shinto sanctuaries were furnished with an Inner Sanctuary, where a Buddhist cult was observed, while the front sanctuary was left comparatively intact. This syncretistic religion was an extension of the Buddhist communion to Shinto deities and at the same time an adaptation of Buddhism to the native religion.'[2]   Thus the encroachments of Buddhism were by no means confined to doctrine. Most of the Shinto shrines came to be served by Buddhist priests who introduced the use of images, incense and an elaborate ritual. Only in the two great shrines of Isé and Idzumo were the ancient Shinto rites maintained in tolerable purity. For many

[1] It should be remembered that it was not the non-theistic Buddhism of the earliest phase of that religion which was introduced into Japan but Buddhism in its Mahayana form.
[2] Anesaki, p. 137.

centuries most of the Emperors, though high priests
of Shinto, assumed the Buddhist tonsure.[1] Some of
them abdicated their imperial rank and divine status
and entered Buddhist monasteries to seek salvation.
For eight reigns, from 1465 to 1687, even the Oho-
nihe ceremony, the Coronation ceremony, the greatest
of all Shinto rites, was in abeyance.[2] Ryobu, or
Mixed, Shinto had a great vogue till the Revival of
Pure Shinto in the eighteenth century. Thus, for a
thousand years, Shinto barely existed except in
combination with Buddhism. As we shall see, even the
Revival failed to achieve a complete disentanglement
of Shinto from Buddhism.[3] The Japanese found it
easy to be Shintoists and Buddhists at one and the same
time, as the Chinese have been able to be followers of
Confucius, Laotze and Buddha simultaneously. What
saved Shinto from extinction was its connexion with
the ruling house—the conviction that the Emperor
was a descendant of the Sun-goddess, who had commis-
sioned him to rule the land.

The reasons why Buddhism was so successful in its
appeal to the Japanese people were many and may
be briefly indicated. Buddhism was intrinsically
superior to Shinto, which had no system of theology
or philosophy and whose gods were either vaguely
conceived or thought of as little superior to mankind.
Buddhism, on the other hand, offered gods who were
the very embodiment of infinite compassion, and by
means of its schools of philosophy it supplied an
intellectual justification for its creeds and dogmas.
Shinto had neither creed nor dogma. Its followers

[1] E.R.E., XI, p. 471.   [2] Aston, S.W.G., p. 364.
[3] When Revon (E.R.E., I, p. 455) speaks of Ryobu as ' only a
shadow cast over Japan from the continent,' he uses an unfortunate
metaphor.

were unable to give a reason for the faith that was in them, whereas Buddhism had an elaborate system of theology, dogmatics, exegesis and apologetics. The intellectual superiority of the new faith was apparent to all cultured minds. Further, Shinto was a nationalistic religion, whereas Buddhism expounded a true universalism. With the introduction of Buddhism, the Japanese learned for the first time of a religion which looked after the welfare and salvation of all beings without respect to clan or nationality. ' Shinto is bounded by Japan in time and space, but Buddhism embraces the universe and stretches its claims . . . from eternity to eternity.'[1] Again, Shinto had nothing to say about the life hereafter. It was content with the world we see and hear and touch. But Buddhism offered men a blessed hereafter to be enjoyed with their fellows in Buddha's Paradise. Buddhism had in the life hereafter a field which Shinto had never entered, and it occupied it with its doctrine of many heavens and many hells.

The astute compromise, by which the Shinto gods were made incarnations of Buddhist deities, contributed to the success of Buddhism. This policy, together with the missionary zeal of the monks, brought over the common people, who felt that they were not asked to abandon the gods of their fathers. The new deities were the gods they had always worshipped, albeit under other names. They could become Buddhists without ceasing to be Shintoists. ' The emotions which belonged to Shinto were thus heightened and broadened. No demand was made for a change in the emotions, but their object was transformed. No longer did reverence and dependence

1 Knox, p. 82.

attach themselves chiefly to nature, for the artistic production of man took its place. Shinto was not deserted, but it was turned to account.'[1]

On the material side, the superiority of Buddhism was equally manifest. Its temples were much more splendid than the Shinto shrines and their worship was much more imposing. Buddhism had what Shinto lacked—a splendid cultus, made impressive and beautiful by fine statues and works of art and all the aid which artistic ceremonial could give. Knox thus describes the contrast felt in passing from a Shinto shrine to a Buddhist temple. ' Instead of the simple *tori-i* are towering gateways, elaborate, ornate, with immense guardian statues, and within are a large and complicated structure and elaborate worship : gongs, bells, incense, revolving libraries, pagodas, sacred wells, drum-towers, images, pictures, carvings, litanies, and companies of tonsured monks. There are monasteries, nunneries, schools for priests, assembly rooms for congregations, holy days and seasons ; magnificently illuminated copies of sacred books with everything for the satisfaction of the intelligence, the emotions, and the will.'[2]

Buddhism had the further advantage of enjoying the prestige which attaches to a higher type of civilization. It, therefore, contributed to the material well-being of the Japanese as well as to the satisfaction of their religious cravings. ' Buddhist propaganda worked in association with the Government in educational work, in the relief of famine and pestilence, distributing medical materials and despatching physicians in company with preachers. These were received by the people with admiration and gratitude,

[1] Knox, p. 88.   [2] Ibid., p. 81.

both towards the State and towards religion. In short, the work of civilizing the country and promoting charitable work lay mainly on the shoulders of Buddhist- workers.'[1]

To return to a point already mentioned in this chapter, the fundamental reason why Buddhism triumphed in Japan was that its acceptance was inevitable when, in the seventh century, the Japanese assimilated so rapidly the civilization of China. ' Old things passed away, and the leaders of the people turned eagerly to the treasures of the continental enlightenment—science, philosophy, art, architecture, medicine, law, literature, poetry, etiquette, highly-organized society and government, to set down at random a few of the elements which impressed the Japanese . . . They reformed their government, instituted a system of education, changed their social organization, turned with eagerness to art, and . . . revolutionized their whole life.'[2]   For them, in those days, there was no escape from the argument that if they wished to be civilized they must adopt the religion upon which the entire civilized world was based.

In the next chapter we shall trace the process by which Shinto, almost absorbed and forgotten in victorious Buddhism, regained for a short time its ascendancy.

[1] Anesaki, p. 83.   [2] Knox, pp. 85f.

CHAPTER IX

THE REVIVAL OF SHINTO

DURING the seventeenth century there was a revival of national consciousness among the Japanese people and an attempt was made to promote the study of Japanese literature and learning, which had long been neglected in favour of Chinese studies. Pioneer work was done by Keichu (1640–1701), who deciphered the archaic orthography of the *Manyo-shiu*, which had long been neglected. His labours were continued by Mabuchi (1697–1769). Attention was thus turned to the study of Japanese history and gradually the idea took shape that the golden age of Japan was before the introduction of Chinese civilization, which had brought with it nothing but declension and corruption in every sphere. This patriotic reaction led to a religious movement known as the ' Revival of Pure Shinto.' Its greatest leaders were Motoöri (1730–1801) and Hirata (1776–1843). Their aim was to establish again a form of Shinto purified from all such foreign adulterations as Buddhism and Chinese philosophy, which they regarded as the work of demons. They proclaimed that such a purified Shinto was the only ' Way ' which the Japanese could rightly follow, since it was the only ' Way ' original and indigenous to Japan, and was, therefore, naturally adapted to her people.

Motoöri and Hirata were learned scholars and voluminous writers who gave themselves to the study of the ancient Shinto writings. Motoöri was thus able to point out that the *Nihongi* made certain concessions to Chinese philosophy. These accretions he stigmatized as ' philosophic terms utterly unknown to the Japanese, . . . the inventions of ignorant men who, instead of accepting with faith the true traditions which had been handed down from the beginning of time, endeavour to discover explanations for what man with his limited intelligence can never comprehend.'[1] The *Kojiki*, which betrays less Chinese influence than the *Nihongi*, was accepted by Motoöri as a reliable record of primitive Japan. He wrote a commentary on the *Kojiki* which runs to forty-four printed volumes.

Motoöri, having adopted this point of view, set himself to answer all the objections which might be advanced against the credibility of the *Kojiki*. To the objection that the *Kojiki* could not be a trust-worthy record in the case of events which took place centuries before the introduction into Japan of the art of writing, Motoöri replied that tradition was better than written records. When the inconsistencies and absurdities of the contents of the *Kojiki* were men-tioned, he replied that the very inconsistencies were a proof of the authority of the record, ' for who would have gone out of his way to invent a story so apparently ridiculous and incredible ? '[2] To the objection that the early records of Shinto contain no ethical teaching, Motoöri replied that only a naturally depraved people like the Chinese need ethical systems. As for the Japanese, they were so divine that they might safely be left to follow their own instincts. Among them

---

[1] Quoted from Satow by Knox, p. 69. We owe our knowledge of this Shinto revival to an article by Satow in the *Transactions of the Asiatic Society of Japan* for 1875.
[2] Satow, cited by Knox, p. 70.

evil did not develop till after the introduction of Chinese ethical systems. In short, Motoöri's ' contention was that the Japanese and their Shinto, when purged of all foreign accretions and influences, represented the pure, and therefore the best, inheritance of humanity from the divine ages.'[1]

Hirata's apologetic for Pure Shinto follows pretty much the same lines as that of Motoöri. He had, however, more propagandist zeal than his predecessor and composed forms of prayer suitable for the use of reformed Shintoists in private worship.[2] The following passages from his writings are worth quoting as revealing his chauvinistic spirit. In the first passage he is discussing the various theories of the origin of the heavens and the earth.

' Our country, owing to the facts that it was begotten by the two gods, Izanagi and Izanami, was the birthplace of Amaterasu, and is ruled by her Sublime Descendants for ever and ever, as long as the universe shall endure, is infinitely superior to other countries, whose chief and head it is ; its people are honest and upright of heart, and are not given to useless theorising and falsehood like other nations, and thus it possesses true and correct information with regard to the origin of the universe. This information has descended to us true and unaltered from the age of the gods, and unmixed, even in the slightest degree, with unsupported notions of individuals. This indeed is the genuine and true tradition. The Chinese accounts sound as if based on profound principles, and one fancies that they must be right, while the Japanese accounts sound shallow and utterly unfounded in reason. But the former are lies while the latter are truth, so that, as time goes on and thought attains greater accuracy, the erroneous nature of these falsehoods becomes ever more apparent, while the true tradition remains intact.'[3]

1 Anesaki, p. 308.
2 The curious may find one of Hirata's prayers and a note on his conception of prayer in E.R.E., X, p. 191.
3 Satow, cited by Knox, pp. 72f.

'The two fundamental doctrines are: that Japan is the country of the gods and her inhabitants are the descendants of the gods. Between the Japanese people and the Chinese, Hindus, Russians, Dutch, Siamese, Cambodians and other nations of the world there is a difference of kind, rather than of degree.'

'The Mikado is the true Son of Heaven, who is entitled to reign over the four seas and the ten-thousand countries.'[1]

In spite of the fact that monotheism has never found a congenial soil in Japan, Hirata tried to find in Pure Shinto some unitary force which lies behind all the varied manifestations of the many *Kami*. He declared that 'the object of fear or worship in foreign countries is known by several names, the Supreme Being, Sovereign Ruler, Imperial Heaven, or Heaven. He is none other than our Heavenly *Kami*, who dwells in Heaven and governs all the affairs of the world.'[2]

In short, Hirata claimed that Shinto was the only true religion; that all others are false; that the Japanese people and the Mikado are the special objects of divine favour, because they stood in a right relation to the Creator and Ruler of the universe, who has created, guided, cherished and strengthened them through all the ages.

The movement for the revival of Pure Shinto was doomed to failure. It was a reactionary attempt to put back the clock by returning to the primitive simplicities of Shinto, whose development had been arrested a thousand years before when Buddhism and Chinese culture entered Japan. It was as though civilized England had been asked to return to the worship of Thor and Odin.[3] On paper the leaders of the movement were able to disentangle Shinto from

---

[1] Satow, cited by Hume, *The World's Living Religions*, p. 167.
[2] Quoted in E.R.E., VI, p. 294.
[3] cf. Miss Trood's *The Religions of Mankind*, p. 111.

its foreign accretions but in practice they could do little. At one point, however, their propaganda bore fruit. Their insistence on the old belief of the Emperor's divine descent and status helped to raise the question why the Emperor should be kept in seclusion in the old capital of Kyoto while Japan was ruled by the Tokugawa Shoguns in Tokyo. Thus Pure Shinto contributed to the movement which led to the Restoration of 1868, when the Shogunate was overthrown and the Emperor became actual as well as theoretical ruler of the land.

One early result of the restoration of the Emperor to power was the re-establishment of the ancient Department of Shinto Rites (the Jingikwan). ' The Department was given the highest position among the government offices, and Shinto was proclaimed the national cult or State religion. This meant at the same time a vigorous suppression of Buddhism, because it was a foreign religion and had flourished under the protection of the Shogunate Government. All the privileges granted to the Buddhist clergy were abolished and a large part of the properties belonging to the Buddhist institutions was confiscated. A reign of persecution was started. Buddhists were driven out of the syncretic Shinto sanctuaries which they had been serving for ten centuries or more. Buddhist statues, scriptures and decorations in those temples were taken out and set on fire or thrown into the water. The " purification " of the Shinto temples was achieved and the severance of Buddhism and Shinto ruthlessly carried out, thus bringing to an end Ryobu Shinto, which had ruled the faith of the nation for ten centuries.'[1]

[1] Anesaki, pp. 334f.

But the movement for the revival of Shinto was too artificial to last for long. The Government could not make its decrees effective and was compelled to modify its policy. It began to realize that the complete suppression of Buddhism was neither desirable nor possible, provoking, as it did, the Buddhists to zeal and united action. In 1877 the Buddhists were granted autonomy and began to recover many shrines, while the common people still clung to their habit of favouring both forms of worship. During the eighties Christianity, another rival to Shinto, was making its influence felt. When, therefore, in 1889 a new constitution was promulgated, it gave liberty of conscience to all religions. The Constitution of 1889 contains the following provision : ' Japanese subjects shall, within limits not prejudicial to peace and order, and not antagonistic to their duties as subjects, enjoy freedom of religious belief.' When in 1899 the officials of the most famous Shinto shrine, that at Isé, petitioned the Government to be considered no longer as forming a religious body but as an association for performing rites in honour of the Emperor's ancestors and for conducting patriotic ceremonies, their request was granted. As Dr. Kato remarks, this gave State Shinto ' a sphere of independent existence quite different from that of the foreign religions ' and furnished it with ' an asylum in which, under the protective ægis of the political power of the secular Government, it is safe from interference by its two religious rivals.'[1] The status of Shinto was thus gradually lowered until under the Shrine Laws of 1900 and 1913 Shinto shrines came under a sub-bureau of the Department of Home Affairs. ' Thus subsided the frenzy of Shinto revival.

[1] Kato, p. 210.

THE REVIVAL OF SHINTO 103

Even the most fanatical of Shintoists recognized the
infeasibility of their plan, and the artificial injunction
of religious and moral teachings proved a failure.
Besides the fundamental error in the attempt at
restoring the old theocratic régime, the causes of the
failure were two-fold : one, the tenacity of Buddhist
faith among the people at large, and the other, the
question of the freedom of conscience, which was
called forth by the discovery of the surviving Catholics
and the new start of Christian missions.'[1]

It is not easy to define the content of the State
Shinto which has been established and also secularized
by the Government. It differs from the Shinto of the
Kojiki and the *Nihongi* ; and from the Shinto of the
scholars of the Eighteenth-Century Revival ; and again
from Sectarian Shinto. According to a competent
observer, who has spent many years in Japan, Western
scientific knowledge has, for the educated classes, so
dissolved the primitive animism of Early Shinto that
little remains except ' a vague belief in the existence
of the souls of Emperors and of the heroes and heroines
of past and present ages. This particular belief,
however, is encouraged by the punctilious performance
of the old state " ritual," and by the almost compulsory
reverence paid to the souls of departed Emperors and
to the souls of soldiers who have died for their country.
The belief is found not to be incompatible with
monotheism, atheism or agnosticism.'[2]

[1] Anesaki, p. 336.
[2] R. D. M. Shaw, *Enlightenment and Salvation*, p. 28.

CHAPTER X

SECTARIAN SHINTO

SOMETHING should be said about Sectarian Shinto which stands outside the pale of State Shinto. Between these two forms of Shinto the Government has long drawn a distinction. It regards the sectarians as forming genuine religious bodies in the same way as the Buddhists and Christians, whereas, as we have seen, State Shinto has been secularized. Like Christianity and Buddhism, Sectarian Shinto is controlled by the Bureau of Religions, while State Shinto comes under the Department of Home Affairs.

According to Dr. Kato, there are thirteen Shinto sects now in existence and officially recognized by the Government as religions on the same footing as Buddhism and Christianity. Some, he claims, have existed from ancient times; others arose during the Tokugawa Régime (1600-1868); others came into existence in the Meiji Era (1868-1912). Professor Anesaki points out that 'a rich soil for spiritual turbulence is found in the field of Shinto religion, partly because it appeals most to the instinctive aspects of a religious mind and partly because its unorganized form is favourable to any variety of ideas and practices.'[1]

In point of fact, Sectarian Shinto owes its greatest impulse to popular teachers, who appeared in the first half of the nineteenth century. They were often simple peasants and yet Shinto owes to them a notable

[1] Anesaki, p. 397.

revival, though they were poles apart from such scholars as Hirata and Motoöri, who led what is technically known as the Shinto Revival. Most of these popular leaders ' derived their inspiration from occult practices prevalent among the mountaineer priests, whose formal affiliation to either Shinto or Buddhism was only a matter of convention . . . These teachers and their followers cherished certain kinds of faith peculiar to themselves, and some of them were men of intense religious experiences. They represented the crude, but comparatively pure, religious spirit buried in the heart of the people[1]; their religion had remained beneath the surface during the reign of perfect stability, when the government and Buddhist authorities kept strict vigilance over religion and made any new move well-nigh impossible. Now, when the Tokugawa régime began to give way to various agitations, these popular religions proceeded to appear in public and finally to achieve an independent growth. Some of these popular religious teachers organized their followers by more or less formulating their teachings, affiliating themselves to Shinto.'

' Besides these religious fraternities for mountaineering pilgrimages, there appeared from time to time teachers of popular religion who inspired their followers by their own faith, independent of any official religion. They worked among the people without any formal ordination, or authorization, and often were persecuted on that account by the Buddhist priests as their illicit rivals. These teachers appeared mostly in localities where the Buddhist priesthood was indolent.'[2]

[1] R. D. M. Shaw (*Enlightenment and Salvation*, p. 28) puts the point another way by saying that the Sectarians ' are much nearer to the animistic stage.'   [2] Anesaki, pp. 310f.

The Sectarians often manifested discontent with the prevailing social and political régime. In their prophetic utterances some of them warned their followers of an approaching world change. There is, so to speak, a messianic element in their teaching. The new age will dawn if only men will abandon doctrinal subtleties and establish a religion of the pure and simple in heart. This sense of a great approaching world change has led some to suspect Christian influence at this point. The practice of mental healing, which is prominent in the Tenrikyo and other sects, exhibits some kinship to Christian Science. Some of the sects manifest a propagandist spirit and an approach to universalism and are, in these respects, non-Shintoistic. Something may now be said about the more important of the sects.

The Kurozumikyo (kyo means ' teaching,' ' doctrine ') was founded by Kurozumi (1779–1849). He was a simple, pious peasant whose deity was the Sun-goddess. ' The deity for him was the source of light and life, with whom we should be in perpetual spiritual communion through prayer and devotion. Human life, according to him, amounted to nothing but a realization of our intrinsic connexion with the cosmic vitality. This communion he called iki-toshi, i.e. " penetrating into life " or " pervaded by vitality." The chief way of realizing this penetration was " inhaling " the divine vitality by facing the sun in the morning and praying to the Sun-goddess. Kurozumi applied this and similar methods to therapeutic purposes, attributing his healing power to the divine vitality with which he was inspired and endowed by the Great Deity. This attracted to him many followers ; but his moral influence cannot be neglected. He regarded the utmost purity and a life of diligence and honesty as the first condition of securing the divine grace. Indeed, his faith in his Great Deity was so personal and intense that his religion verged on monotheism pure and simple.'[1]

The Tenrikyo (' Teaching of the Heavenly Reason ') sect was founded by a woman named Miki (1798–1887) of Yamato. In the year 1838, she announced that ' she was possessed by a god who called himself the Lord of Heaven and commanded her whole family to dedicate everything to his cause for the sake of mankind.' Her generosity reduced her family to poverty and so alienated their sympathies from her that her only sympathizer was her daughter. After the death of her husband, ' the mother, having forsaken everything of the world, now appeared as the apostle of the new religion which amounted to the belief in the God of Heaven and to the admonition to purify oneself. The human being, she taught, is the abode of divine charity and the only obstacle is greed together with all that it implies. Get rid of every stain of the soul, restore its original purity, everything will follow and end in happiness—union with the divine spirit. The mother and daughter effected mental cures in the firm belief that all ills and maladies were simply due to illusion caused by greed and associate vices. This teaching gradually attracted believers and in the course of further fifteen years the mother was regarded by her followers as the saviour of the world, which was to undergo a remarkable transformation because of her appearance. They were persecuted, but the following grew, so that she was a very prominent religious leader in her province at the time when the

[1] Anesaki, p. 315.

Tokugawa fell and the new government was inaugurated. Thenceforward, the last twenty years of her life were a period of the rapid growth of her religion, in spite of persecution renewed under the new régime.'[1]   She taught that there was a spot near her home where the divinity would descend to consummate the transformation of the world.   The place was called ' The Terrace of Nectar ' and is now covered by a gigantic temple.   It is claimed that the Tenrikyo is the largest Shinto body to-day.   The photographs reproduced by Professor Anesaki (Plate XXII), showing the crowds assembled in 1926 to celebrate the fortieth anniversary of the death of the foundress of their sect, are worthy of attention.

The Konkokyo (' Teaching of the Golden Light ') sect was founded by a peasant named Kawade (1814–1883).   He laid emphasis upon the necessity of sincerity of heart.   Like the Tenrikyo, the Konkokyo uses mental healing and inculcates direct spiritual communion with the deity.   The former is most influential among the peasants, the latter among the masses of the industrial towns.[2]

The Omotokyo (Omoto means ' the Great Fundamentals ') is a quite recent sect, which is not recognized by the Government and is, indeed, severely persecuted by the State authorities.   According to Professor Anesaki it is ' the crude expression of religious aspiration . . . pretending to reveal the mysteries of life, especially of the national life of Japan, the divine mysteries long obscured and suppressed by the wanton tyranny of the privileged classes since the very beginning of the "Age of the Gods."   The movement

[1] Anesaki, p. 314.   See also p. 371.
[2] See further Anesaki, p. 372.

was started by a woman fanatic, who believed herself to be the prophetess of the gods and wrote down the divine messages in automatic handwriting during more than twenty years of her " god-possessed " life. Gradually, dissemblers and fanatics flocked around her, and when, during the World War, uneasiness about the outcome of the war began to overtake some people, especially military and naval men, the propounders issued various predictions warning the nation against a foreign invasion. The predictions, though always worded in ambiguous terms, amounted to saying that the whole country would be devastated and that the only place saved would be Ayabé, a little town in central Japan, destined to be the centre of the new world-order ruled by a theocracy of the Great Fundamentalists. Besides appealing in this way to the apprehensive fear as well as to the patriotic pride of the people, they practised a kind of mental cure by hypnotism combined with exorcism, which they call " divine possession," a practice common to all Shinto movements.'[1] In spite of persecution the Omotokyo appears to flourish and claims to have followers in China and Korea.

[1] Anesaki, pp. 397f.

CHAPTER XI

PRESENT POSITION AND FUTURE PROSPECTS

A QUESTION of much interest and no little difficulty is that of the future prospects of Shinto. Criticism of Shinto is an easy task. It has often been pointed out that it has no dogmas, no theology, no metaphysics, no ethics, no contribution to make to the solution of the social problems thrust upon Japan by the industrialization of her life, no missionary spirit,[1] no saints and martyrs, no hope of a glorious immortality, though it believes in the survival of the dead in an underworld. On many of the fundamental themes of religion it has nothing to say. For this reason it has not been possible to include in the present work a treatment of the Theology of Shinto. It is noteworthy that the *Encyclopædia of Religion and Ethics* has not been able to include articles on Shinto's contribution to such doctrines as Salvation, Righteousness, Grace, Atonement. The positive defects of Shinto are as glaring as its deficiencies. Its polytheism is apparently incurable ; its stories of the gods are fairy-tales ; its cosmogony belongs to the childhood of the race ; it has always been a national religion in which membership is defined by nationality[2] ; it is barren of spiritual

[1] It is claimed that Sectarian Shinto is making many converts, but, as we have pointed out above, this is one of the respects in which Sectarian Shinto is non-Shintoistic.

[2] For an ingenious and ingenuous defence of the nationalism of Shinto, see Kato, p. 88 and pp. 202ff.

power as is shown by its history and its lapse into inertia after its task of restoring the Emperor to power had been accomplished.

Yet there is something to be said on the other side. There is definite religious value in Shinto's insistence on cleanliness and purity. If Shinto has been non-missionary, it has never proselytized and never persecuted. Its fortunes may be interlocked with those of the Japanese peoples, but it ' is unique among the religions of the world for the contribution which it has made to the political theory and national stability of its own adherents.'[1] It has inculcated, as perhaps no other religion has done, the ideal of self-sacrificing service on behalf of the nation. But, above all, Shinto deserves credit for its insistence on the truth that nature is a manifestation of the Divine. ' No race, ancient or modern, seems to have had a keener appreciation of nature than the Japanese, or to have been more inspired by it in the formation of its religious ideal. The Japanese were inclined toward this state of mind by the very character of their country—a land full of contrasts, at once tragic and smiling, terrifying and gentle, stern and mild ; refusing man much and giving him more ; shaken by volcanoes, devastated by floods, swept by tempests, and at the same time rich in hidden resources and dazzling splendours, fertile in crops and beauties. Such a land was bound to make the deepest impression on an intelligent, artistic people inclined by their innate goodness of heart to look on the benefits of nature rather than on its scourges, and to see in the beauty of their country a constant reason for gratefulness to the gods . . . Throughout the whole course of their

[1] Hume, *The World's Living Religions*, p. 146.

history, from primitive times to our own days, the Japanese appear as essentially charmed with nature, wonderfully gifted to understand it as artists, and predestined to love and adore it.'[1]

Discussions of the future prospects of Shinto often forget the following points. (1) It is kept alive among the masses by those festivals and pilgrimages which are so dear to their hearts, and by their quasi-religious veneration of the Emperor. (2) Sectarian Shinto, which is a popular movement and has left the educated classes untouched, has still a great appeal and preserved the name of Shinto together with a few of its main features. (3) The life of Shinto is prolonged by the Japanese tendency to eclecticism—a tendency which has been accentuated since Japan was opened to Western ideas. 'In what religion then do I believe ?' asks Professor K. Kumé. 'I cannot answer that question directly. I turn to the Shinto priest in case of public festivals, while the Buddhist priest is my ministrant for funeral services. I regulate my conduct according to Confucian maxims and Christian morals. I care little for external forms, and doubt whether there are any essential differences in the *Kami's* eyes, between any of the religions of the civilized world.'[2] (4) In spite of all its intellectual limitations, Shinto still has a great emotional appeal. The veteran scholar, Inazo Nitobe, in his recent work *Japan, Some Phases of her Problems and Development,* speaks of Shinto as 'the *ensemble* of the emotional elements of the Japanese race.'

Logically the secularization of State Shinto means

[1] Revon, in E.R.E., IX, pp. 233f. See p. 234 for a striking account of the love of nature in the hearts of the common people to-day.

[2] Quoted in *The Missionary Message,* p. 78 ; cf. Anesaki, p. 9.

that as a religion it is now extinct. It now exists purely as a civic institution. The priests of all Shinto shrines, of which there are said to be some 50,000, are now *in jure* secular officials under government control. Many Japanese accept this secularization of Shinto as an accomplished fact and are content for it to survive as a secular system for fostering patriotism and loyalty. For this party ' Shinto is not a religion at all, but is, rathei, a repertory of State ceremonials and national morality or ethics, the former being conducted generally in Shinto shrines, while the latter is inculcated in public schools through the canon of the Emperor's Meiji's Edict on the Education of the young generation of Japan, promulgated in 1890.'[1] Similarly, Baron Keiroku Tsuzuki says, ' Shinto is a crystallized system of rites for the veneration of the personalities closely connected with our existence and our national history—in other words, a systematized and complicated form of taking off our hats before the emblems of our ancestors and national heroes.'[2]

These secularists, into whose souls the acids of modernity have bitten so deeply, naturally prize Shinto as a means of keeping up the patriotic spirit of the nation and of preserving respect for authority. Every revival of patriotic feeling gives them an opportunity of emphasizing their principles. They use official Shinto as a weapon for repressing ' dangerous thoughts.' They urge that every Japanese ought to support State Shinto and take part in its ceremonies, even though he is, for example, a Christian in enjoyment of that freedom of conscience guaranteed by the Constitution of the country. According to them, even a Christian ought to support State Shinto, which is

[1] Kato, pp. 208f.　[2] Quoted in *The Missionary Message*, p. 74.

8

not a religion but a part of the nation's public institutions. Thus Professor S. Tachibana says, ' as it is
the great way of the Empire, all Japanese, ancient
and modern, in spite of different creeds, must be
Shintoists.'[1] Professor Anesaki appears to doubt the
bona fides of this party and dislikes their secularism.
He says ' there is much artificiality in the conventional
interpretation that this Shinto is not a religion, but
there is some truth too, both because the exponents
of the theory are anything but religious and because
their sincerity is not unquestionable.'[2]

In spite of all difficulties the Government clings to
the hope which led it to separate Sectarian and State
Shinto—the hope that the latter may prove to be a
national cult of loyalty in which even Buddhists and
Christians may take part without prejudice to their
own religious convictions. In recent years it has
taken not a few steps to intensify the cult. The
coronation of the Emperor Hirohito in 1928 ' was an
occasion for the most thorough diffusion of State
Shinto ideas and practices of recent years. We had
hymns to the Emperor, prayers in all the schools of
the Empire, facing Isé when the Emperor went into
the sacred enclosure, all sorts of ceremonies at the
State and local shrines, and tons of literature inspired
and sent out by the Government.'[3] Special honours
were paid to the Emperor Meiji (d. 1912), by ' the
erection and integration in the life of Japan of the
Meiji Shrine in Tokyo. This is the focus of the

[1] E.R.E., V, p. 499.
[2] Anesaki, pp. 407f. See further the article by D. C. Holtom,
' The Political Philosophy of Modern Shinto ' in *Transactions of
the Asiatic Society of Japan*, Vol. XLIX (1922) Part ii.
[3] Dr. C. W. Iglehart, cited by Braden in his *Modern Tendencies
in World Religions*, p. 146.

national cult on its recreational side, of national games,
&c. ; and shares with Isé the chief place in the linking
up of State Shinto with the army and national policy.
There is being built up over the country a network of
local shrines to the Emperor Meiji.'[1]   The Rescript
issued by the Emperor Hirohito at his coronation is
noteworthy :

> Our Imperial Ancestors having laid the foundation of the
> Empire in pursuance of the divine command have reigned
> over and governed their people with benevolent care.   The
> forefathers of our subjects have on their part, been constant
> and loyal in their service.   Consecrated by the ties which
> unite the Sovereign and the subject, as Father and child,
> our Empire has developed a character unique and unrivalled
> in the world.[2]

More recently the War in Manchuria has intensified
devotion to State Shinto as the religion identified with
Japanese culture and national aspirations.   The
observer cited above for the events in 1928 says every
regiment ' lines up before the Meiji shrine before
leaving for Manchuria.   The local shrines have never
been so busy since the Russian War.'[3]   In 1920
Marxian Communism began to take root in Japan and
won some amount of support among the labouring
and student classes, many of whom show a tendency
to abandon religion in any form, owing to their conviction that Shinto, Buddhism and Christianity have
alike failed to meet the needs of the people involved
in the industrial struggle.   By 1931 two definitely
anti-religious unions were founded to preach that
religion is the opiate of the people.   Their activity has
led the Government to encourage all forms of religious

1 Dr. C. W. Inglehart, cited by Braden in his *Modern Tendencies
in World Religions*, p. 146.
2 Cited by Shaw in his *Enlightenment and Salvation*, p. 21.
3 Braden, *op. cit.*, p. 174.

activity and teaching ' on the assumption that religion was an upholder of the *status quo*, and that it would help to make loyal citizens, who would resist the encroachments of Communism.'[1]

Japanese Buddhists and Christians are not altogether happy about the Government's policy. ' The fact that the state ceremonial invokes largely the same gods as Sectarian Shinto and uses much the same ceremonial, makes the government's claim seem a specious one to Buddhists and Christians, a device by which constitutional freedom of worship may be theoretically maintained while carrying on the ancient religion of Japan.'[2]   Apparently Roman Catholic Christians have received something like formal sanction to their taking part in State Shinto rites.   At any rate, ' a case has been made out by Catholic theologians for permitting Japanese converts to take part in traditional observances to the Mikado, because of the formal and patriotic character of the proceedings and because of the Byzantine precedent.'[3]   Protestant Japanese Christians find themselves in a more difficult position and it stands to their credit that through the National Christian Council of Japan they issued more than one protest against the war with China and spoke boldly of the invasion of Manchuria as ' a violation of the covenant of the League of Nations.'   The great Christian leader, Kagawa, gave open expression to

---

[1] Braden, *op. cit.*, p. 139.   See also Basil Mathew's *World Tides in the Far East* (Chapter V) for a vivid account of the political and other parties in the Japan of to-day.

[2] Ibid., p. 146n.

[3] Nock, *Conversion*, pp. 229, 301.   Nock points out that by the time of Claudius the worship of the Emperor in the Roman Empire had become little more than an outward sign of loyalty involving little sentiment ;   and that some of its outward manifestations passed into the customs of the Byzantine and Papal courts.

his sympathy with the Chinese. The Buddhists, apparently, remained silent at this time of national crisis. It is too early as yet to predict what the final result of the Government's policy will be. A recent Japanese writer points out that modern conditions are weakening the hold which the worship of ancestors has upon the minds of the Japanese, and that this may have important political results, since the devotion of the Japanese people to the Mikado is based on ancestor worship. ' Even the Imperial House,' he says, ' would be powerless against our changing concepts of ancestor worship.'[1]

Other Japanese do not take kindly to the secularization of State Shinto. They are as patriotic as the secularists but they are more religiously minded. In the fight between religion and non-religion they are on the side of the gods. They are not satisfied with a purely humanistic interpretation of the universe and feel that morality cannot be divorced from religion, or it will be left without stable foundations. They are aware of the defects of Primitive Shinto but they claim that in the course of its history it has outgrown them. They do not accept the thesis that its development has been arrested. Dr. Kato appears to belong to this group. His book is a protest against the general attitude of Western students of Shinto who regard it as belonging to the past. ' In my opinion,' he says, ' Shinto is by no means to be classed with the religions of the past. It is alive—nay, it is very vitally active in the ethico-religious consciousness and national life of the patriotic Japanese of to-day. Shinto is, in truth, like Christianity, Buddhism or Islam, one of the world's living religions.'[2]   He offers

---

[1] Cited by Braden, *op. cit.*, p. 140.   [2] Kato, p. *ii*.

the following definition of Shinto : ' The vital essence
of Shinto manifests itself in an expression of that
unique spirit of the national service of the Japanese
people, which is not only mere morality but is their
religion, culminating in Mikadoism or their peculiar
form of loyalty or patriotism towards the Emperor,
who is at once political head and religious leader
in a government constitutional yet theocratico-
patriarchal.'[1]   He is emphatic in his insistence that
Shinto is not a mere system of morality but is a living
religion, though at the same time he makes Emperor-
worship the central feature of his reconstruction, which
is little more than a modernization by rationalization.

    Most European scholars regard Shinto as a lifeless
relic of the past, which has no living power to compete
with Buddhism and Christianity. Aston does not
hesitate to say that ' Shinto is doomed to extinction.
Whatever the religious future of Japan may be, Shinto
will assuredly have little place in it.   Such meat (sic)
for babes is quite inadequate as the spiritual food of a
nation which in these latter days has reached a full
and vigorous manhood.'[2]   Professor Krause declares
that Shinto ' has now little more than an archæological
interest.'[3]   Such judgements appear to be a little too
peremptory, not to say superficial. They do not
sufficiently differentiate between the vital essence of
Shinto and those defects in it which are so easily
pointed out for criticism.

    A much more sympathetic judgement is that of
Professor G. W. Knox, whose experience as a Christian
missionary in Japan gave him a truer insight into the
psychology of her people.

[1] Kato, p. 208.   [2] Aston, S.A.R.J., p. 81.
[3] In Clemen's *Religions of the World*, p. 260.

'Shinto is more than a code of ceremonies, for in a
true sense, it embodies the religion of the people. . . . The
legends, cosmology, and pseudo-history are not the religion,
and its power is not in dogmas nor in forms of worship ; it
is a spirit, the spirit of Old Japan.

'The essential fact in Shinto is the religious patriotism
of the people. To them Japan is a divine land, and their
devotion expresses itself in loyalty to the Emperor. With
this loyalty combines a faith in the continued existence of
the heroes of the past, and their inspiration of the nation
in its toils and aspirations. The Emperor is not a god, in
our modern sense, nor is the land an abode of supernatural
beings, but, true to the ancient meaning, " divine " signifies
superior, worshipful, that to which one bows in adoration
and gives himself in consecrated service. The belief in the
continued power and inspiration of the spirits of the past,
though taken over from the Chinese, has become essential,
yet rests on no argument and is embodied in no dogma. It
has no clear vision of a heaven or hell, or of any state of
rewards and punishments. In emotional content it can
scarcely be distinguished from our Western reverence for
the saintly and heroic dead, while its influence on the
living is akin to the patriotic feelings excited by our
recognition of a precious inheritance in the patriots of ages
past. Thus Shinto is witness to an abiding reality. Though
its forms perish, its substance remains beyond the reach of
hostile criticism and argument. If its doctrine be vague,
and its emotions with difficulty described, this is because
it belongs to those powerful feelings which are only partly
differentiated, and in this it remains a true representative
of primitive religion, of the simple feelings which persist,
their interpretation being restated with man's progress in
knowledge. Shinto will survive—not in its dates, nor its
genealogies, nor its theory of the descent of its sovereign
from Amaterasu, nor in its legends and cosmology, but in
the affections of the people, their trust in the national powers
and destiny, and their confidence that there is a something
more than their present strength and wisdom which directs
and aids and on which they may rely. The " something
more " may receive new names, but the faith will abide
while Japan works out a future greater and more glorious
than the fabled Age of the Gods.'[1]

So far we have had in mind the future prospects

[1] Knox, pp. 77ff.

only of State Shinto, by which is meant the ceremonial of the court, together with the cultus performed by Shinto priests, at shrines dedicated to Shinto deities. What are the prospects of Sectarian Shinto ? Most discussions of the prospects of Shinto leave out of account the Shinto sects. This is almost inevitable, for until recent years the West had little detailed knowledge of the Shinto sects, which have never been studied as carefully as the Buddhist sects of Japan. Scholars assume, perhaps too easily, that Sectarian Shinto cannot have a future because it appeals almost exclusively to the ignorant masses. Even Japanese scholars speak disparagingly of it. Thus Professor K. Ashida says that the Sectarians, though they claim the name of Shinto, really have little connexion with the ancient system of that name. They simply continue the ' old superstitious practices under the guise of Shinto worship.'[1]   There is, as we have seen, some truth in this criticism but it cannot be accepted as a final judgement. Professor Anesaki's treatment of the Sectarians is much more sympathetic and is due, no doubt, to the fact that he is himself a Buddhist. He feels that Sectarian Shinto meets a need felt by the lower classes, who appreciate its direct appeal to the heart.

The wise prophet will hesitate before he predicts the early disappearance of either State or Sectarian Shinto.   As Professor A. N. Whitehead so well says, ' In any survey of the adventure of ideas nothing is more surprising than the ineffectiveness of novel general ideas to acquire for themselves an appropriate emotional pattern of any intensity.   Profound flashes of insight remain ineffective for centuries, not because

[1] E.R.E., VII, p. 484.

they are unknown, but by reason of dominant interests which inhibit reaction to that type of generality.   The history of religion is the history of the countless generations required for interest to attach itself to profound ideas.   For this reason religions are so often more barbarous than the civilizations in which they flourish.' [1]

[1] *Adventures of Ideas*, p. 220.

APPENDIX I

LITERATURE

ANESAKI, M. . *History of Japanese Religion* (London), 1930).
Written in fluent English. Thoroughly scientific in its treatment. The only book in English dealing with Sectarian Shinto on any scale.

ASTON, W. G. . *Shinto, the Way of the Gods* (London, 1905).
Still the best book in English on the subject. Noteworthy for its copious translations and native illustrations.

ASTON, W. G. . *Shinto, the Ancient Religion of Japan* (London, 1921).
An abridgement of the above. Too slender to be of much use to the student.

ASTON, W. G. . Article on Shinto in Volume XI of the *Encyclopædia of Religion and Ethics* (Edinburgh, 1920).
Breaks very little new ground.

GRIFFIS, W. E. . *The Religions of Japan* (London, 1895).
A pioneer book, still useful and noteworthy for its sympathetic insight.

KATO, G. . . *A Study of Shinto* (Tokyo, 1926).
Written to correct what the author thinks are the mistaken views of Western scholars and to set forth Shinto as a living religion. Nothing like so readable as Anesaki. Dr. Kato has read widely in the history of religions but his power of analysis is not equal to controlling and presenting the mass of material he has collected. His book will confuse a beginner but may be useful to the advanced student who can make the necessary allowances for Dr. Kato's apologetic motive.

Knox, G. W. . *The Development of Religion in Japan* (New York and London, 1907).
A well-written treatment of the subject.

Revon, Michel . *Le Shinntoïsme* (Paris, 1907).
Noteworthy for the care with which it distinguishes between Primitive and Syncretistic Shinto. More in touch with recent work on the scientific study of the history of religions than Aston.

Schurhammer, Georgb (S.J.) *Shin-To ; The Way of the Gods in Japan, according to the Printed and Unprinted Reports of the Japanese Jesuit Missionaries in the 16th and 17th Centuries.* (Bonn and Leipzig, 1923).
Printed in English and German in parallel columns and profusely illustrated.

The student will find useful treatments of Shinto in Moore's *History of Religions* (Edinburgh, 1914) ; Hume's *The World's Living Religions* (Edinburgh, 1924) ; and in Cave's *Living Religions of the East* (London, 1921).

There are many articles dealing with the various aspects of Shinto in the *Encyclopædia of Religion and Ethics.* Those by Revon are particularly good. The article ' Japan ' will give the student a succinct account of the geography, ethnology and history of the land.

As their titles indicate, the works by Anesaki, Griffis, and Knox deal with Buddhism and Confucianism in Japan, as well as with Shinto.

A useful feature of Aston (S. W. G.), Kato, and Anesaki is their illustrations, which are generally wanting in books dealing with the history of religions.

APPENDIX II

INDEX

CPSIA information can be obtained
at www.ICGtesting.com
Printed in the USA
BVOW08s2053280118
506565BV00001B/57/P